For
2010
Carla
Flowers and
memories
Sia
x.

grandiflora
arrangements

grandiflora
arrangements

saskia havekes & gary heery

LANTERN
an imprint of
PENGUIN BOOKS

contents

introduction

With luck on my side and the world glittering in front of me, my love of flowers has taken me towards fulfilment of a passion, leading me down paths of endless surprise, gilded with adventure and good fortune. It always surprises me that there are people who don't have a passion in life. Personally, I have a lot of trouble controlling my consuming passion for my work; my family will verify this without hesitation. The introductory quote in Eric Hansen's book *Orchid Fever* (Vintage, 2001) by Joe Kunisch, a commercial orchid grower in New York, states, 'You can get off alcohol, drugs, women, food and cars, but once you're hooked on orchids, you're finished. You never get off orchids – never.'

Such single-minded devotion to flowers can blur the line between love and lunacy. For instance, in the 17th-century, tulip madness or 'tulipomania' gripped the Netherlands. This craze eventually swept Europe and fortunes were made and lost in the blink of an eye. Speculating on rare bulbs and the flowers they would produce predated the furore that was created during the dot.com boom of the 1990s. During the peak of tulipomania, citizens kept bulbs in bank vaults for security; I completely understand this sort of passion, but cannot explain why or how one becomes so enveloped by it.

I seek beauty in everything, and see flowers and art linked through creativity – flowers can be the inspiration for great works of art and the artists themselves are often interested in creating wonderful gardens. My love of flowers has taken me to many places. For me, flowers are a celebration and affirmation of life and colour; their optimistic faces are both strong and fragile.

Each and every flower has a personality and form of its own – just like humans, some are extraordinary. I can see them, gazing and pert, always ready to reach their full potential. It is bland to have them all standing perfectly in a row; much more interesting to see the backs and their other angles. Sometimes it can feel overwhelming to have masses of flowers waiting to be reshaped and placed. In this initial stage they can feel like opponents – then when they do what you expect they become friends.

My concept of 'leisure time' in the conventional sense is rather non-existent. Bringing beautiful flowers to others has become my life's vocation. This involves long hours, hard work and low remuneration. Florists never become millionaires. You have to love what you do to justify the way it consumes most of your waking hours.

The word 'grandiflora' seems rather self-explanatory. Meaning 'large flower' in Latin, it is used in the names of a great many plants, trees and flowers to refer to their larger specimens. My most inspirational flower, *Magnolia grandiflora*, influenced me when naming the business over ten years ago. It was the only name I considered. Most people associate the shop and the work we do with a form of largesse.

I get great inspiration from vistas I observe in the world; flowers of all shapes and varieties; and colours in the landscape. Anyone driving between Sydney and Melbourne at the right time would have happened upon vast stretches of the weed Patterson's Curse, which flowers an ecclesiastical purple for kilometres over the rough terrain; or paddocks of golden canola under cultivation; or the great stretches of yellow wattle on either side of the Hume Highway in spring.

I created a number of the arrangements here from such sources of inspiration in my everyday life.

Flowers are ephemeral, a 'happening' if you're lucky enough to be there at the right time, with no promise of them being there days later – a kind of 'catch-us-if-you-can!'. My aim is to catch and hold them for as long as possible, then put them where they can be astonishing and remarkable, for other people to share the experience. I like the fact that in my job I get to start at the very beginning – a customer comes in with an idea in a jigsaw-form that I can help to complete. Often they know the practical components, the type of architecture and the light to be used. They have in mind the general look, colours, shape and fragrance that they are after. I know what flowers will be available and source them in the right quantities and best quality, then I see the project through to completion.

In the course of our work, my faithful team and I are shown an amazing assortment of venues in which floral arrangements are to be placed, usually for specific events and occasions – their function being to beautify, impress and improve. I then have to devise an appropriate container, and out of the raw materials available in that particular season, create an arrangement that the client feels satisfies their vision. In the flower business, buyers are looking for consistency, innovation and healthy, dependable flowers; they have an insatiable appetite for something new or out of season.

Most things in life respond to care and this certainly applies to all things floral. The more care that is given to an arrangement, the better it looks and the longer it lasts. The blooms need their water changed and their stems cut regularly or they become unattractive, smelly, and don't usually last for long.

Starting a job begins with a 4 a.m. visit to the flower markets. The market morning is a treat and great source of inspiration. One must be in close contact with suppliers and growers beforehand: placing orders; checking on availability; and confirming quality. A common scenario for a major migraine to occur is a grower being unable to fulfil a promised order. Dependency on the weather and reliable transport, if an order is being shipped from another state, makes their job difficult. Sometimes lateral rethinking of an arrangement is needed to come up with alternatives.

The growers I deal with are wonderful people – very hard-working and always doing their best to please us demanding florists, who in turn are trying to please our clients. Growers start their day at midnight and end at midday, primarily to suit other people.

Flemington Market in Sydney is a hive of industry from the early hours of the day until around 9 a.m. I love the atmosphere – its energy is reminiscent of the streets of New York – people on the move doing things, quantities of produce being shifted around, bought and sold, all ready to provide me with daily motivation for my work.

The perfect bloom demands a discerning eye – any flower is beautiful if it has grown in an extraordinary colour or to an altered size. Sometimes growers can produce that unusual twist I always look for. I especially love flowers that look as though they have literally been picked from a garden, and sadly wonder whether finding these will always be possible. Lack of space and water, plus the increasing trend towards cultivation in controlled environments, already means that fewer smaller growers are appearing at the markets with odd little gnarly things; increasingly the flowers available are more mass-produced. In this changing environment, it is a treat to find independent suppliers. To me, it is the ultimate in time wealth to be able to spend a whole day gardening.

It is an art to choose and prepare flowers for their big moment. Each occasion is assessed in days of concentrated, arduous attention, to help the bloom reach its perfect state for its big performance; on days like this, I feel like the ringmaster.

To some, flowers are at the luxury end of the scale, but to many others, like me, they are a necessity, a daily enjoyment that lifts the soul. Some customers would prefer to eat less in order to buy more flowers. Busy inner-city dwellers scoop them up at the end of the week and relax with them over the weekend. People often pick their flowers one by one with an idea in mind, while others ring and ask us to do it for them.

It is so important to remind ourselves from time to time that each flower is beautiful in its absolute raw state. People needn't be daunted by complicated structures and terrifying botanical names, and should take a moment to observe each specimen for its intrinsic value. A good florist is someone who can put you at ease and open your eyes to the idea of appreciating simple flowers arranged together in their most harmonious combinations.

An elderly client grew up in Katoomba, and when daphne flowered in winter, her entire house would be filled with it. This seems so decadent to us in the shop, as daphne is now so expensive and hard to come by. She still sends her family cuttings to remind them of their childhood.

Preparing arrangements for people staying in hospitals is a good case in point, as they are often the recipients of floral arrangements and bunches of cut flowers. Flowers are sent to cheer them up, congratulate, improve morale, or as an expression of care, concern, pride or happiness. Most hospitals have a limited assortment of water containers, often resorting to jars and plastic buckets. We decided to always send some kind of water-containing vessel with every arrangement sent to a hospital because

I've seen flowers received in this situation being fitted in the most unsuitable containers. It's a bit like trying to fit feet into shoes that are too small and tight. Overly large floral displays are also hard to handle in a hospital. Sometimes small plants in pots are a good, lasting gift as the patient can take them home and the maintenance is usually stress-free. Very sick patients don't appreciate hectic arrangements with vibrant colours. I have found that using quiet colours and a well-chosen selection of quality or single orchids are good choices.

A bride's mother didn't want to have any blossom at her daughter's wedding. To her, it was hideous to have such an ordinary, tough bloom at a wedding ceremony, having grown up on a large country property where blossom was the only thing to flower in such barren, dry land. After working with flowers for fifteen years, it changed my perspective on the way I see blossom.

Contemplating my last ten years of running Grandiflora, I am able to reflect on the contribution that many of my colleagues and clients have made in shaping what has evolved into our signature look today. As part of this process, accepting that there are other ways of seeing and doing have been great tools for building a fresh, positive and stable working environment. Openness to opinions from clients can be a vehicle for developing new ideas.

Most recently, I was asked to make a casket cover for a Russian poet. The flowers requested were sunflowers, camomile and wheat. These are not flowers usually chosen by us for funerals, but after an intense discussion with my client I could absolutely understand what she wanted to convey. The result made her burst into tears. Painfully, I knew I'd done my job.

At Grandiflora, we love to workshop materials and thoughts in a group, drawing ideas from what flowers might be in season and available in sufficient quantities. When arranging flowers for an occasion it is important for us to take into consideration the following factors: the available budget; what mood the guests will be in; the time of day the event will be held; the theme; the general colours being used in the setting; whether it will be formal or informal; an image of the desired mood and atmosphere and the shape of the tables. All these elements help to determine the choice of flowers, structures, containers and foliage. Anything too large in the centre of the table can be a hindrance at a sit-down dinner if the eye contact for guests is interrupted.

From sketching out our initial concepts we step into the logistical side of things, a much overlooked area. Finalising the structure, or really pulling arrangements together, makes or breaks a job. What drives me to make sure any flower moment is prepared properly is the trust people bestow on me. I often pinch myself at such times, remembering to thank in my head the Grandiflora team, and the growers, clients and my family who entrust me with this task – this propels me forward.

I once read that creativity is made up of ten per cent concept and ninety per cent hard work – this really applies for us here! Anyone who has worked extensively with flowers will understand the hours and physical labour that come into play to make the most of the experience of flowers. When preparing flowers I often visualise the intense amount of rehearsal and focus dancers have to endure to discipline and train their bodies and minds for their performance. I find that meditation on this is a source of great strength. The secret is to make it all look effortless.

Most importantly, there is an expectation (on the part of ourselves and our clients) for us not to be completely predictable and to always strive to push a request just that little bit further visually. That could mean adding something unexpected as a surprise or paring an arrangement back to a Zen-like statement of simplicity. My job is never about working to an exact formula.

In essence, we are the bloom wranglers. In working with flowers I often think about the psychology of the bloom and what it is that makes me tick – do I want to find the perfect flower or am I trying to please the client? Ultimately, I believe the flower is the driving force, that and making sure it looks perfect on the day.

Many of the arrangements featured in this book were created by Grandiflora from flower-inspired statements given to us by some of our clients, colleagues and friends. We hope you enjoy the results.

autumn

in season

march beehive ginger, belladonna lily, cattleya orchid, gardenia, hippeastrum in pots, hyacinth, hydrangea (autumn), oriental lilium (also sold as Casablanca lily), pink torch ginger, roses (including 'Angel Face', 'Iceberg' and 'Mount Shasta'), tulips (including parrot-style), waterlily

april *Curcuma alismatifolia* (also sold as Siam tulip), cyclamen, hyacinth, king protea, lisianthus, oriental lilium (also sold as Casablanca lily), pomegranate, roses (including 'Iceberg'), rose hips, tulip (including 'Maureen')

may arum lily (white and 'Green Goddess'), chrysanthemum (disbud-style), kale, kangaroo paw, tulips (including 'Maureen' and parrot-style)

also in autumn amaranthus, bouvardia, buddleia, chrysanthemum, crabapple, dahlia, delphinium, nerine, orchids (especially cattleya, cymbidium and slipper), peppercorn (berry), red hot poker, firewheel, sunflower

'From the tightest of buds to an explosion of colour and personality, these ever-moving and twisted tulips never fail to delight. Their daily changes are for the better, until the petals drop; sad only for a moment, until the next bunches arrive.'

MARTIN BOETZ

Despite its seeming simplicity, this arrangement was actually very challenging. Tulips are so luxurious in their abundance; here I used ten bunches of large cream tulips, such as 'Maureen', with most of their foliage kept intact.

STEP ONE
First, working in bunches, run the tulip stems under fresh water to clean them of any trapped soil; this prevents the water in the vase from becoming muddy. Cut 10 centimetres off the base of the stems at an angle; this re-opens the stems.

STEP TWO
Place one bunch (approximately ten stems) of tulips on a slight angle at the edge of the vase, then keep adding to this cluster, bunch by bunch, until the bowl is full. The total number of tulips will depend on the size of the bowl.

STEP THREE
Pull the occasional tulip up a little higher than the others, as a slight unevenness across the top adds interest and undulation.

Longrain Restaurant, Surry Hills.

'I just love the sheer beauty (often extravagance), creativity, fragrance, surprise and thrill of receiving a bunch of flowers. One of the things I love most is the colour. My arrangement is inspired by the beauty of autumn flowers. Like Keats in his poem *Ode to Autumn*, I too appreciate the "mellow fruitfulness" of the colours of full-blown, dried-out flowers, the way they fold and fade as they illuminate the grass, blossoms and leaves, and the asymmetry of autumn.'

JUDITH COOK

Judith Cook is a flower addict like me! At Grandiflora, we were amazed by the beautiful sketch she drew of her ideal *Ode to Autumn* arrangement. Together, we tried to replicate it here. Judith added the final touch of the dried grass, which really made this arrangement sing. This eclectic display of autumn is actually quite dense and abundant in combination.

STEP ONE
Start by placing approximately eight blue hydrangea stems in a tall jar, half-filled with water, then add a large branch of red flowering gum (*Eucalyptus caesia*) to one side.

STEP TWO
To add height and stability, place a green gum nut branch at the back of the jar, along with one large stem of green/yellow cymbidium orchid.

STEP THREE
Then push a purple vanda orchid (with its water vial attached) in to the right of the jar; this way it has its own water source, as it only has a short stem.

STEP FOUR
Add the individual stems of black 'Baccara' roses, 'Webber' tulips, red or orange crucifix orchids and a hint of lime-green chrysanthemum. As a finishing touch, a few bare branches of red-barked dogwood (*Cornus alba*) were placed so they poked out from the arrangement, adding a wispy element.

Judith Cook's own oil jar.
Home of Judith Cook and Grant Matthews.

12

'My favourite orchid is the cattleya.
I am wowed by its tropical opulence.'

DR PATRICK TISMO

STEP ONE
Cut a few centimetres off the stems of
five white cattleya orchids; this re-opens
the stem, allowing it to take up water.
I cut them to 20 centimetres, as visually
I like to only ever have relatively short
stems for these orchids.

STEP TWO
These vases were a particularly favourable
shape for this type of orchid, as they have
a wonderful cupped shape with a tight
opening to hug the flowers into position.

STEP THREE
Each stem was placed by first observing the
direction of the flowers, how they would sit
in the vase and their most favourable angle
in these containers. It is important to keep
the blooms upright and not at all facing
down, so they don't look floppy and tired.

Penthouse of Dr Patrick Tismo and Jeff Connor.

STEP ONE

I started by placing a cylindrical glass vase half-filled with water inside a large French ceramic confit jar.

STEP TWO

Next, I chose about five stems of firewheel tree (*Stenocarpus sinuatus*) with their flowers still mostly in bud. I retained some of their leaves so the arrangement wouldn't look too de-nuded. It was lovely to include blooms at various stages of their development in the arrangement.

STEP THREE

I then placed the stems in the centre of the container, letting the flowers trail down over the left-hand side.

The design of the firewheel tree flower before it bursts open gives me so much evidence that man can never replicate nature. Then the surprise of seeing the flowers burst into their crazy, spider-like form is an even greater example of this. It's a native tree that hasn't truly been cultivated or utilised in flower decorating yet, although the flowers were made famous by Margaret Preston in her art.

19th-century French confit jar from The Country Trader.

'For me, flowers evoke a multitude of emotions and memories, punctuating the stages of my life. My affair with flowers started at a young age in Maleny, Queensland. I picked bunches of forget-me-nots from our garden, much to my mother's dismay, herself despising the 'weed'. I in turn, not caring for the thorny roses that struggled while my faithful blue flowers thrived.

In my arrangement, I chose the phalaenopsis orchid: bold and voluptuous, it is the ultimate in decadence. I juxtaposed this with its antithesis, the waterlily — bashfully beautiful, reticent to open and expose herself.'

LUCINDA JOHNSON

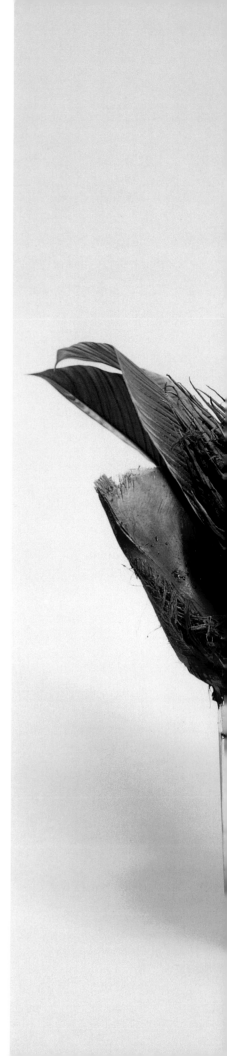

STEP ONE
Place a short palm husk to the left-hand side of a trough vase three-quarter filled with water; this will act as a block to secure the large, variegated green and yellow dieffenbachia leaves which frame the back of the arrangement.

STEP TWO
Add about seven bold green leaves such as spathaphyllum to the back of the trough, fanning them out to form a backdrop. Place three spiky burrawang pods (*Macrozamia communis*) nestled in amongst the husk and leaves.

STEP THREE
Next, insert approximately 20 stems of waterlilies to the front, towards the right-hand side of the trough.

STEP FOUR
Carefully add approximately three stems of phalaenopsis orchids, with their stems cut low, in amongst the groups of waterlilies so that they trail slightly down over the edge of the trough.

STEP ONE
Cut two large mallee gum branches such as *Eucalyptus pyriformis* or *E. youngiana* to 40 centimetres, then trim off some of the foliage.

STEP TWO
Place branches in a tight-necked round vase, half-filled with water, at right angles to each other, with the gum nuts resting on the rim of the vase.

STEP THREE
Take a cluster (approximately five pieces) of bark and break them into various lengths, then slot them into the vase, interspersed with the gum branches so they stand upright throughout the centre of the arrangement.

STEP FOUR
Place three large burrawang pods low in the arrangement, adding an intriguing element to capture the eye.

The mood for this arrangement was set by the owner of the premises. He likes his arrangements to be placed in glass only, favouring complete simplicity with a strong sculptural edge. He prefers not to overwhelm people in his retail space with large blossomy blooms. Fortunately, these two very chunky gum stems formed themselves into a strong shape when placed in this vase, while the burrawang pods at the centre of the arrangement anchored the gum. It is certainly an interpretation of an Australian landscape with a sophisticated edge. This arrangement has very good longevity — approximately three weeks. The water needs to be changed every three to four days as the bark tends to discolour it.

Blinds by Bayliss.

STEP ONE
Fill a large, wide tapered vase three-quarters full with water, then add a base of variously sized and shaped tropical leaves, with some larger velvet philodendron leaves to the left and a group of dark philodendron leaves to the right.

STEP TWO
When the vase is quite full, select five lotus pods and insert them at varying heights into the right-hand side of the vase, in front of the group of philodendron leaves.

STEP THREE
Place 7–9 anthurium flowers, trimmed to 35–40 centimetre lengths, in the centre of the vase, between the two groups of leaves. They should sit along the tops of the leaves, nestled against the lotus pods to create the illusion that they are growing naturally with the leaves and pods in the vase.

The philodendron leaf is an absolute favourite of mine — I love its silk-fabric quality and its amazing, wide, rounded heart-shape. When using them in an arrangement, I always try to exhibit them as prominently as possible, placing them over the top of the other base leaves. It was important here to create a lot of bulk and movement.

This is a typical, elegant white and green arrangement from Grandiflora. It offers great longevity — many people even like to keep the lotus pods in a separate vase to dry after the leaves and anthuriums have died.

'I chose this plant, a succulent, because its very
nature reflects the qualities I most admire in people:
generosity, life-giving, resilience, intelligence,
wholesomeness, consistency and earthiness.'

KYLIE KWONG

STEP ONE
This installation was a touch experimental.
I first removed 8–10 flapjack succulents
(*Kalanchoe thyrsiflora*) from their pots
and placed them on plastic lining in a very
large (1 metre wide) black wooden dish.

STEP TWO
I then took a few dried wood rose stems
(*Merremia tuberosa*), cleaned of their
thorns and foliage, and placed them in
amongst the succulents. This took some
time as the wood rose stems were very
curvy; it was quite a challenge to place
them mostly facing towards the front,
but the result was pleasing.

Billy Kwong, Surry Hills.

Set against fabric supplied by Akira Isogawa, the colours
in this arrangement are warm and almost autumnal,
while the various shapes and textures are very complementary.
The chrysanthemums at the front of the vase replicate the
beautiful chrysanthemum shapes in the fabric behind.
This is a typical arrangement which could be sent as a gift
from Grandiflora to my sister Anna-Maryke — a flower
enthusiast, who loves eclectic bouquets such as this.

STEP ONE

This arrangement is not placed in
a vessel; instead it is standing alone
on its stems. This is called 'straussing'
and is a more traditional floral technique.
The preparation for this bouquet is very
important. All the flowers used have first
been stripped of their foliage. This bouquet
was created in the hand, starting with
two bunches of 'Hot Chocolate' roses,
which were first stripped of any thorns,
damaged petals and foliage.

STEP TWO

Approximately six dahlia blooms were
fed in randomly throughout the roses.
I then added three groups of amaranthus
to the left, centre and right of the
arrangement.

STEP THREE

Next, I inserted a few key flowers,
such as the three chrysanthemums,
which I hid in areas throughout the
bouquet. Cyclamen was clustered at the
front, tucked in between the dahlias and
chrysanthemum. Coneflower seedpods
(*Echinacea purpurea*) and amaranthus
seed heads were placed in the centre
as a textural element. A few feathery
carnations were placed to the far
left and in the front of the bouquet,
to add texture, colour and intrigue.

STEP FOUR

Finally, I added a few croton leaves towards
the base of the bouquet, creating a feeling
of strength. An athertonia leaf was placed
at the base. I couldn't resist tying the
arrangement with a very luxurious long
velvet ribbon.

'Chrysanthemum' fabric in background
courtesy of Akira Isogawa.

'I love this quote, by the infamous Anonymous, as it indicates the depth of emotion I feel for these glorious and impeccable flowers.

I would rather have one little rose
From the garden of a friend
Than to have the choicest flowers
When my stay on earth must end.'

BELINDA SEPER

I fell totally in love with David Austin roses when I first saw them. A lot of people don't understand them at all. They think they look half-dead or drooping. It's true that they're not very long-lasting and they tend to start losing their petals before they open right up, but that's part of their beauty as well. They're like really big eggs with large feathers wrapped around the outside of them.

These roses are very special – they're layered, fabric-like and highly specialised, and to me, they complement Belinda's style. The suggestion of fabric in the background also seems to emphasise this association.

Belinda loves all the powdery-coloured roses and the lushness of using roses in one single colour. Here, their tone also matches the contemporary vase I have selected to offset the old-fashioned nature of these roses.

STEP ONE
David Austin roses are quite wayward, so it helps to use a narrow vase to hold them up, with the buds spilling over the rim. This vase has a 15–20 centimetre opening, so the base flowers must form the support for the arrangement. The leaves will cloud the water, but they also help to form a great structure for the arrangement in the vase. Either change the water regularly or use an opaque vase as I have here.

STEP TWO
Using a total of 6–8 bunches of David Austin roses, start forming the base with two bunches at the front of the vase and two placed towards the back. Either pull the rubber band on each bunch quite close to the base of the actual flowers to create a chunky bundle or tie them with a piece of soft cord. Rest the necks of the roses just above the rim of the vase.

STEP THREE
You then need to be quite gung-ho about chopping off a lot of the stems and pushing them down into the vase. Although stripping the leaves from the stems makes the roses last a bit longer, keep some of the leaves intact as these anchor the stems in the vase.

STEP FOUR
Once you have your base, start feeding separate stems in over the top of the base roses to form layers; these must be stripped of their foliage and thorns or they will tangle with the existing stems. I like the look of new buds appearing through the old flowers.

It is quite hard to obtain such a huge old-fashioned sunflower now, the type you see, field after field, in France. This one was grown by an Italian gardener who had to keep the cockatoos from its seeds so we could cut it in time to be photographed.

STEP ONE

This sunflower image was created by hand-pinning each petal around the sunflower's seeded face and placing it in the centre of a French-bleached oak table.

STEP TWO

A wire armature was made around the outside of the table. This formed a base structure to weave and thread autumn foliage into.

STEP THREE

I then fed twelve long pieces of wild hops (a weed also known as turkey rhubarb) and two bunches of red-tinged nandina foliage (approximately 10 stems) through this wire structure, creating a foliage bed to surround the edges. The arrangement was then shot from above.

'Sunflowers grown for oil were a part of my childhood in northern New South Wales; following the sun, they sleep at night. In my second life, as an antique dealer in Sydney, I search for form and wit. The sunflower lies yellow against the soft brown of a French-bleached oak table, with its daisy-petal pattern. These are the autumn colours I crave to experience on my regular stays in Europe. Horizons grow as life passes.'

GEOFF CLARK

19th-century French-bleached oak table from The Country Trader.

Due to their colour and size, these vanda orchids ('Robert's Delight') are well sought after and hard to obtain. When we acquire them in plant form, they are very quick to sell; we even have waiting lists. One Valentine's Day we hung twenty plants in the shop window and they were all sold before midday. The cut flowers have great longevity and can last up to a month.

The linear nature of the bamboo is quietened by the shape of the soft, round flowers. There's a lovely sense of movement, as the bamboo limbs, which are still attached to the trunk, jut up into the air to create an element of intrigue and give the piece its striking line.

STEP ONE
This arrangement makes an ideal table centrepiece. Take an 80 centimetre piece of bamboo trunk with three holes cut at irregular intervals into one side, then lay it on a table.

STEP TWO
Cut three stems of vanda orchids so that the length of the stems allows the flowers to sit along the top of the bamboo trunk, then place them in water vials. Place the water vials in the three the illusion that the orchids are growing out of the bamboo. The bamboo can be re-used; simply replace the flowers. I also added a few firewheel tree leaves (*Stenocarpus sinuatus*) along the top

Every so often, one of our private suppliers of orchids and unusual leaves kindly provides us with a surprise box of treasures; this amazing combination was one of them. The little refined cream *Aerangis citrata* orchids only flower once a year and this would be the quantity we receive at that time, here in this single arrangement. I often fantasise about pinning them to a bride's hair as a hairpiece. There are two species of petite orchids, *Aerangis citrata* and *Dendrochilum cobbianum*. Using a stem of zygopetalum orchid flowers, I added a little bit of purple to the centre of the arrangement, which was essential to break up all the brown and green tones. It's also lovely to see some of the leaves kicking up and others trailing down.

STEP ONE
As the stems of all these orchid specimens are very fine and the cube vase used is relatively large, I pushed a handful of begonia leaves into the base of the vase to create pockets to feed the various orchids into.

STEP TWO
Starting with approximately ten stems of paphiopedilum orchids, I cut the stems to approximately 20–30 centimetre lengths then fed individual stems in at various heights.

STEP THREE
A delicate single stem of small, straight zygopetalum orchid was added next, placed in the centre. A few stems of *Aerangis citrata* were then added to the right and left of the arrangement.

STEP FOUR
Next, an entire bunch of trailing *Dendrochilum cobbianum* petite orchids was added to the front of the vase as a feature, cascading out over the edge and onto the table.

STEP FIVE
Finally, I added a few bold *Alocasia gutlata* v. *imperialis* accent leaves to the front left and right-hand sides of the arrangement.

When someone commented that this arrangement, with its long, flowing tail of medusa leaves (*Anthurium* 'Medusa'), looked like a parrot, I was amazed — any such resemblance was quite unintentional. Parrot tulips are probably more for the flower connoisseur; they're wrinkly and quite awkward and floppy to use in an arrangement. The reward is in their amazing colour and movement — the parrot tulips I used here were particularly green, but usually they are more obviously yellow and red. I love the way their feathery petals transform and fade as they open. I also like how this arrangement is set against slate; its chalky texture works well with the leaves and the dark vase.

Most of the arrangement has been pulled forward in the vase, so that it's not left sinking in the middle. While the leaves on the right provide a visual bulk, the medusa leaves offer a sense of release from the structure of the main arrangement. All these leaves have great longevity. You could leave the arrangement for quite a few weeks, just replacing the tulips, which are available throughout autumn, winter and spring, and should last for a week.

STEP ONE
I bundled together three bunches of parrot tulips in the hand, leaving most of their leaves intact. I then placed the tulips in a medium-sized round vase half-filled with water.

STEP TWO
I then placed a big 'Pigskin' philodendron leaf on an angle behind the right-hand side of the tulips. It's an incredible, very strong leaf which almost acts like a board supporting the tulips because they have very fragile stems. I then placed an *Anthurium 'Medusa'* leaf to the right of the arrangement, sitting behind the large 'Pigskin' philodendron leaf.

STEP THREE
Next, I placed a few green philodendron leaves to the right side, and added a few long *Anthurium 'Medusa'* leaves, which I allowed to trail out from the vase behind them.

'Nature has been a never-ending source of inspiration for Dinosaur Designs. Flowers, in particular, are a magical world of colour, perfume, texture and form. Whether they are bursting out like fireworks or tiny and delicate, boldly sculptural or fragrant and delightful, flowers are always surprising. They can take your breath away with their incredible beauty, or shock you with their unexpected strangeness.'

LOUISE OLSEN, STEPHEN ORMANDY, LIANE ROSSLER

The day we arrived at the Dinosaur Designs studio to photograph these flowers was a memorable one – there was much chaotic joy with many vases, colours and blooms to choose from and all of us working together as old friends who are unanimously flower-crazy. We all had so much joy putting together the final result.

This configuration of vases and plants could be good for a windowsill, mantelpiece or placed down the centre of a drinks table; it is far too tall for a centrepiece for seated guests, as it would obstruct their vision across the table.

STEP ONE
We started by placing this eclectic array of interestingly shaped Dinosaur Designs vases in a disjointed line. Balancing the tall (trimmed to 1 metre) red umbrella tree stems in a strong vase was a good beginning, sometimes the lower berries need to be cleaned off to allow the bare stems to be easily placed in the vase. Keeping these flowers in one group also makes a strong statement. This vase was placed at the back of the arrangement, slightly to the left side.

STEP TWO
Ten stems of helicopter hands (umbrella tree leaf fronds with their leaves removed) were then put into a vase that matched their colour beautifully and placed to the far-right of the grouping. Cut to varying lengths, they have benefited from being inserted with a bit of separation, as this enables you to see through their spiny 'fingers'.

STEP THREE
Three lotus pods were placed in a tall vase with a narrow neck to hold their stems in position; after the other components have died, these can be kept and dried. This vase was placed to the left of the group, alongside the umbrella tree stems.

STEP FOUR
In the centre, to the right of the umbrella stems, six sarracenia pipes were added, cut to varying heights between 40 and 50 centimetres. They have an eye-catching venation and their whiteness creates a striking lift in the centre of the piece. They were placed in a bulbous vase with a narrow neck to support their long stems.

STEP FIVE
A deep red waxy orchid was placed in the foreground, at the neck of a shorter vase, making a wonderful intriguing specimen.

STEP SIX
A selection of unique leaves was then placed between the feature flowers: a group of cordyline leaves, with their wonderful yellow rims, were placed to the left, beneath the lotus pods; alocasia leaves were placed towards the back; and burgundy and green waxy succulent leaves of rhoeo (*Tradescantia spathacea*) were clustered at mid-level.

STEP SEVEN
Finally, several umbrella tree stems were laid along the base of the vases to the front of the arrangement, creating a diversion of linear energy.

Selection of Dinosaur Designs vases.

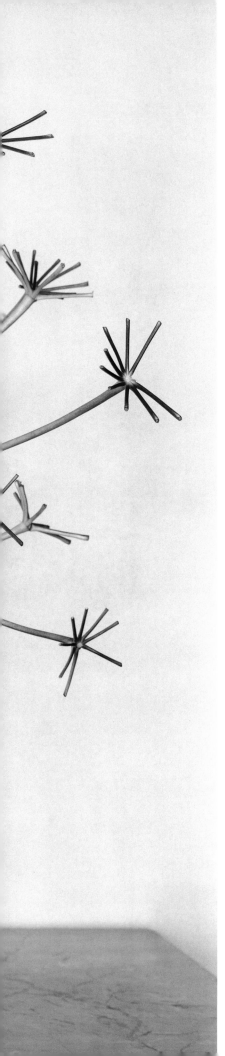

Battery acid vases have become antiques now and I quite like replicating the chunkiness of the solid glass with flowers. When I'm arranging flowers I always have combinations of opposing words running through my mind, like solid and sparse, heavy and light, formal and informal.

Here, I like the way the umbrella tree stem stripped of its leaves looks like little sparklers coming out of the side — it is like a release from the heavier part of the arrangement. Another important point is to use both sides of the alocasia 'Green Velvet' leaves, as I have done here; you can create an interesting energy by turning a leaf back to front or putting it upright.

STEP ONE
I began by placing an umbrella tree branch at an angle on the right side of the vase. This branch had a really thick stem that formed a good structure to feed other things through; it was like the bones of the arrangement. Umbrella trees are pretty boring old plants, but I clipped the leaves off here, leaving the stalks, to change its appearance.

STEP TWO
Next, I added a single gymea lily which I had cut down to 70 centimetres, then placed it at an angle to the left of the vase so that it sat slightly more forward than the umbrella tree. Sometimes the simplicity of using a solitary bloom acknowledges its beauty in amongst everything else.

STEP THREE
I then added approximately five stems of cymbidium orchids. I cut another cymbidium orchid stem in half, then inserted both halves next to each other, placed low at the front of the arrangement.

STEP FOUR
Through the middle, I then fed down a branch of *Eucalyptus youngiana*, to add a rough, contrasting texture.

STEP FIVE
As a final touch, I fed five velvety alocasia leaves through the arrangement; some rising upwards at the back, some facing out to the sides and others facing downwards at the front left-hand side. A large philodendron 'Redwing' leaf was added at the right-hand side.

Elizabeth Bay House, Sydney.

winter

in season

june anemone, banksia, clivia, gardenia, gymea lily, hyacinth, magnolia, tulip (including 'Maureen' and parrot-style)

july arum lily ('Green Goddess'), daphne, gum nuts, gymea lily, hakea, hellebore, japonica (flowering quince), magnolia, orchids, prunus blossoms (such as cherry, plum and peach), sweet pea, tulips (including double cream, 'Queen of the Night' and 'Rococo'), wattle

august arum lily, cherry blossom, daphne, freesia, hellebore, hyacinth, japonica (flowering quince), jasmine, orchids (including cymbidium and slipper), roses (including 'Iceberg'), sweet pea, tulip

also in winter apple blossom, candytuft, camellia, Canterbury bell, cornflower, daffodil, delphinium, holly, jonquil, lisianthus, poppy, protea, ranunculus, rhododendron, smoke bush, strelitzia, succulents, sweet William, thryptomene

'I love the moody seductiveness of the dark purple 'Queen of the Night' tulips. So sensual and elegant to the eye, they look like velvet and emanate such a sense of luxury. Also, they are similar in hue to the skin of eggplant, my favourite vegetable — another reason for their appeal. They remind me of Monet's inspirational garden in Giverny, France, where I first saw them, and I buy them whenever they are available.'

CHRISTINE MANFIELD

STEP ONE
The easiest way to create a bouquet
of these 'Queen of the Night' tulips is
to first strip them of most of their foliage,
then make the bouquet up in your hand
ready to insert into the vase.

STEP TWO
It is best to add a handful of stems at
a time, until there are enough to form
a stunning bouquet. (I used approximately
four bunches here, that is 40 stems.)

STEP THREE
Carefully place the bouquet into a tall
vase then slightly readjust them to
create a pleasingly uneven silhouette.

'Squeezeblack' vase by Orrefors.
Lotus Bar and Restaurant, Potts Point.

There's a brilliant wintry mood to the colours, textures and simplicity of this arrangement. It seemed important to group the two vases together in order to make the arrangement look complete. With their waxy texture, these pink torch gingers are fascinating, they're such a graphic flower with a pretty pale colour. They needed to stand alone in an arrangement, with only a hint of another element to add height and balance. They also look great juxtaposed with dark green leaves. The furry magnolia buds were bound to open within a few weeks, altering the appearance of this arrangement entirely.

STEP ONE
I cut three branches of magnolia to various lengths (approximately 1.5 metres each) then placed them in the larger vase, which I had half-filled with water.

STEP TWO
I then cut six pink torch ginger (*Etlingera elatior*) stems to staggered lengths and placed them at intervals throughout the magnolia.

STEP THREE
I used only three pink torch ginger stems in the smaller vase, as I didn't want it to look overcrowded or overbalanced.

Establishment Hotel, Sydney.

STEP ONE

Half-fill a bucket with water, then place one floral foam brick in the centre of the bucket to form a central bar (or you could use a roll of chicken wire as a structure to prevent the bunches from sinking into the bucket).

STEP TWO

Place 15–20 bunches (approximately 20 stems per bunch) of differently coloured open poppies to each side of the central floral foam, working inwards, until the poppies fill to the centre of the structure. Make sure you push some bunches lower than others, as this creates a more natural undulating effect.

'I like poppies: their exuberant colour, the way they pop and unfurl from their husky ball, their paper-thin bodies that allow light through. More than any other flower, they enter a room like the yellow light from the sun.'

KNIGHT LANDESMAN

Zinc bucket, 19th-century oak Spanish table and 19th-century French pine arch shutter from The Country Trader.

STEP ONE
I began by selecting an eclectic array of resin and glass frosted vases from Dinosaur Designs in colours that complemented the chosen flowers. I then scattered them along the bench, placing them in a line of varying heights to create an unpredictable visual rhythm.

STEP TWO
Next, I trimmed the burgundy cymbidium orchids, with the evocative names of 'Valley Vampire Blood' and 'Khan Flame Lucifer', to various lengths. I placed some orchids in most of the vases and left others empty. By keeping the lower blooms closer to the vase necks, a visual fullness is created.

STEP THREE
Finally, I added some luscious Bourgogne anthurium flowers in a tight cluster to one low vase and placed the vase slightly off centre, drawing the eye in.

Longrain Restaurant, Surry Hills.

'A quote that particularly resonates with me, from Anaïs Nin, is, "There came a time when the risk to remain tight in the bud was more painful than the risk it took to blossom." '

GENEVIEVE FREEMAN

This camellia-filled clam shell is an example of how flowers do not always need to be displayed in vases. To achieve more height in the flowers, it would be an advantage to use a piece of floral foam in the shell, cut to size.

STEP TWO
I clipped two bunches of camellias (with approximately five flowers per bunch) to very short lengths, retaining most of their foliage. I then placed these stems in a large clam shell filled with water.

STEP THREE
Next, I separated the stems from a third bunch of camellias. I poked these stems randomly into the clam shell to give a feeling of height and depth to the arrangement.

How elegant is a camellia? It conjures up memories of my grandmother's garden in Avalon. I remember my great aunts having many marine props around the garden, like this clam shell. When we were children, my sisters and I used to play all sorts of imaginary games there, amongst the camellias, violets and Illawarra flame tree. As we lived in the bush, my grandmother's place was a seaside contrast to our usual playing field. It was my sister Ineke who first opened my eyes to these timeless blooms.

Home of Susan Bowden.

This vase was designed by the French florist Christian Tortu, who is a wonderful source of inspiration. He was the first modern designer to keep flowers in large clusters, together with collars of grouped leaves, fruits and vegetables. Some of the vases he has designed have very unusual shapes, with openings that lend themselves to holding specimens or masses of a specific flower.

In many ways this is quite a simple arrangement to create. What makes it more intriguing is that the hawthorn berry is without its leaf, so the beauty of the berries is on display. I recommend using gloves if you plan to strip away the prickly leaves yourself.

STEP ONE

To create the base, strip the leaves from three bunches of hawthorn berries (*Crataegus*), then bundle them together in both your hands. Squeeze the stems together and feed them into a vase with a narrow neck, leaning them towards the right.

STEP TWO

To give the arrangement its interesting shape, I kept most of the branches gathered together in the narrow neck of the vase, then pushed two or three stems down a bit further, to stagger their heights. This makes the stems appear longer than they actually are, which is more economical than buying longer berry stems.

STEP THREE

Take an extra bunch of hawthorn berry, then feed individual stems into the arrangement. I loosely fed a few sprigs of berries into the top of the vase to create height, then placed others angled to the right-hand side; this gave an unexpected, natural look, as if the arrangement had just been picked from the bush.

Christian Tortu black (cygnet) vase from Macleay on Manning. Medusa Hotel.

STEP ONE

These unruly sweet peas are the true, natural, garden-grown version, with their delicate tendrils still attached. I split three differently coloured bunches of sweet peas between three vases, keeping each arrangement loose and free, rather than compact and dense.

STEP TWO

To achieve this, I placed each stem, cut to different lengths, individually and at varying heights, in each vase until I reached what I felt to be the right balance.

'For me, freshly picked garden roses or sweet peas in a simple glass vase lift the spirit with their fragrance and colour. Flowers help bring the outside in and affect the senses, evoking a mixture of emotions and memories. It is just as pleasurable to give a beautiful arrangement as it is to receive one. Bouquets should be simple; flowers should be allowed to speak on their own!

I am fortunate enough to be surrounded by and appreciate the beauty of nature, especially flowers. This is often reflected in my Collections, where I try and capture the feeling or colour that has been inspired by a particular flower, whether it be the scent, the hue or the texture.'

COLLETTE DINNIGAN

Background fabric and vases courtesy of Collette Dinnigan. French oak Louis XV table from The Country Trader.

Don't be afraid to go into your garden and pick things you wouldn't normally think
of putting into a vase. Be adventurous: get out the handsaw and chop off some cactus
then combine it with a few unusual elements you might get from a florist. At Grandiflora,
we often cut a piece from a potted succulent plant and wire it into the side of a vase
or table centrepiece.

Given the privilege of working with this precious sculptural vase I decided something
whimsical and eccentric would be appropriate – a sort of carnivalé hat! In keeping with
this dynamic spirit, it seemed appropriate to create discordant proportions between
the three elements in the arrangement.

STEP ONE
Cut a long twisted piece of cactus and
then lean it against the left side of the vase,
placing it so that it appears to be growing
naturally from the vessel. When working
with cacti, it is advisable to wear sturdy,
waterproof gloves to protect hands from
the prickles and milky sap exuded by
cacti and succulents such as euphorbias,
which can be harmful.

STEP TWO
Cut three red torch ginger flowers,
then place them at the front of the vase
so they sit protruding slightly from the top,
adding a vibrant burst of vital colour.

STEP THREE
As a finishing touch, place 7–8 furled
leaves of *Calathea lutea* (also called Havana
cigar due to their shape) among the torch
gingers and behind the cactus.

Picasso vase from a private collection.

STEP ONE
Remove the elastic bands from approximately six bunches (about 60 stems) of large cream tulips (for example 'Maureen'). Trim the stems to 50 centimetre lengths.

STEP TWO
Place the tulip bunches on a slight angle, to the left-hand side of a trough vase three-quarters filled with water. Keep adding blooms until the vase is full, pushing the stems so they are standing upright and linear.

'Flowers can always give away the style of a restaurateur, so they must reflect the restaurant. I believe in using only freshly cut flowers, with no arrangement of any sort; just one bunch of flowers (preferably tulips), to soften the room. Nothing too high; trees are for our gardens, not inside restaurants. Tightly closed tulips are my favourite; they have more power.'

MAURICE TERZINI

Icebergs Dining Room and Bar, Bondi.

STEP ONE

Trim the stems of one bunch of rhododendrons (approximately five stems) to 25 centimetre lengths, then place them in a wide, tall vase half-filled with water. Cut one bunch of burgundy magnolia flowers (approximately five stems) to 20 centimetre lengths, then place them randomly around the rhododendrons.

STEP TWO

Take two full stems of *Rondeletia amoena* and place them at either side of the vase so that they sit a little higher than the rhododendrons.

STEP THREE

Push in a large stem of Illawarra flame tree seed pods (*Brachychiton acerifolius*) towards the centre of the vase. Poke in three large pieces of stachyurus, keeping them quite long and wayward looking. Add accents of white daphne throughout the arrangement.

STEP FOUR

As a finishing embellishment, place a single large stem of cattleya orchid in the centre of the arrangement with its stem hidden so it looks as if it's floating.

It was one of those glorious, blue-sky winter's days. The flowers chosen for this arrangement were dictated by the vessel, made of fragile resin with a pansy motif. The combination of colours and textures were selected with the delicate finish of this vase in mind. The burst of vibrancy was reminiscent of a hot summer's day spent sitting by the pool in a pretty pink dress, drinking ice-cold lime juice cordial with a splash of pink grapefruit juice.

Resin vase and location courtesy of Susan Bowden.

'Wombats, kangaroos, wallabies, feral goats and rabbits; our bush block has the lot. Cultivating a garden here, near Mudgee, has been a challenge. Fences are burrowed under and easily hopped over and exotics make irresistible grazing for our furry friends. A few hardies manage to survive their hungry onslaught, but it's the natives that win the battle hands down.

There was a wonderful native nursery where we would often go for stock. One memorable excursion we drove back with close to one hundred seedlings. But as we were powering home, the wheel suddenly broke off the axle. Swerving violently towards a eucalypt, the vehicle spun around before finally it toppled onto its side, covering us in sandy soil.

Thankfully we survived uninjured, as did a handful of plants, including one fragile *Hakea laurina*. As if to celebrate its escape, it has thrived in its home in our garden. Nearly a decade on, it towers about five metres high, erupting each year with spherical pink blooms.'

NELL SCHOFIELD

STEP ONE
I placed 3–4 sprigs of pincushion hakea (*Hakea laurina*), trimmed to 20–30 centimetre lengths, into two smaller water vials to prevent them from leaking into this gorgeous little 15 centimetre-high wooden vase.

STEP TWO
I placed one sprig upright on a slight angle to the right of the vase, then I added another sprig to the left of the vase, placing it so it lay horizontal to the table.

STEP THREE
Finally, I added another small sprig with most of its foliage removed to the centre of the arrangement.

Nell Schofield's own wooden vase.
Rose Seidler House, Wahroonga.

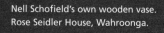

'I work from home as a contemporary art curator and my days are typically long and cerebral: I spend hours on end combining and conceptualising artworks for particular places and contexts. A weekly ritual that gets me away from my desk and out into fresh air is my walk up the alley to Grandiflora to say hello to Saskia. I always come away with flowers, often her oddest and most sculptural ones. Not being from here, I tend to marvel at what the Australian bush can force up from the hard, dry ground into full and fragile bloom: all those exotic botanical specimens that are good at retaining water and the range of outrageous waxy yellow and sticky red phallic forms.

I then carry them home and set them in front of Rebecca Smith's wonderfully fluid wall drawing, made from brightly-coloured sticky tape. At the shop, Rebecca's drawing is never far from my mind and when I return home and set the flowers down, this exchange I have set up – an impromptu choice that blends certainty with instinct – ends up looking just right.

Today, however, Saskia and I decided on something different. We selected tulips and gum stems that mimic the textures of the tape drawing, its wrinkles and ridges, and the way that Rebecca's line curves and doubles back on itself – not unlike the meandering and sinuous curves of the tulip stems as they reach for the light.

We have lived as a family with Rebecca's work for three years now. Physically and literally it lies at the hub of our home and we never tire of its commanding presence. It has become an interior bower as exuberant and alive as Saskia's shop of flowers.'

BARBARA FLYNN

STEP ONE
Take five bunches of tulips (50 stems),
then cut off all the rubber bands.
Group the stems into one large mass.

STEP TWO
Cut all the stems to even lengths (the
exact length will depend on the height
of the vase you are using) and place
them in a vase. Shuffle some of the stems
and blooms to create a visually pleasing
and uneven shape.

STEP THREE
Slide in a few gum stems, kept together
as a group and to the right-hand side
of the tulips.

Elizabeth Bay Tangle, 2003, wall drawing by
Rebecca Smith, coloured sticky tape on wall,
270 × 470 cm.

This arrangement is dedicated to my father, Gerard Havekes. The cordyline, with its spiky leaves, was given to us at the Sydney flower market by a grower, Gary Van Hof, a Dutchman, like my father. I'd asked him for something incredible to use, so he gave me this particularly good specimen. I felt it should be used as one big statement. Finding a flower to go with it was easy in this winter season, as the 'Queen of the Night' tulips offered exactly the right colour. Although we used about eight bunches, it was worthwhile. They needed to be kept clustered in one big group to balance the strength of the cordyline leaves behind. The astonishing shape and size of this date palm stalk with fruit is very rare, and completed the arrangement.

The 'Queen of the Night' tulip is a favourite of mine. They always remind me of the time Dame Joan Sutherland walked into the shop and admired a big vase of tulips — when she asked what they were, I said, '"Queen of the Night".' She then broke into operatic song and, when I inquired what she was singing, she replied, 'The Queen of the Night aria from *The Magic Flute*.'

STEP ONE
Place one large stem of cordyline leaves on an angle at the back of a deep, wide vase three-quarters filled with water.

STEP TWO
Carefully wash the stems of eight bunches of 'Queen of the Night' tulips, as mud often collects between their leaves. Keep most of their leaves on, as they will provide the bulk filling the base of the vase.

STEP THREE
Form one large bunch of tulips in your hand and cut the stems to 30 centimetres, then place the tulips to the front left-hand side of the vase.

STEP FOUR
Using one hand, separate the deep red cordyline (*Cordyline terminalis* 'Nigra') and tulips, then, with your other hand, push a date palm stalk into the centre of the arrangement, keeping it central and low.

Rose Seidler House, Wahroonga.

'The beauty of these phalaenopsis orchids lies in the fact that their stems are relatively short and each bloom is perfect. It was important to have a cavern of leaves running through the centre to create a sense of definition and strength. The venation of the *Alocasia amazonica* leaves seems more prominent when set against these white blooms. The flowers have a butterfly-like quality and so they are commonly called moth orchids. The centre of the flower is reminiscent of a moth's antenna and although its intricacy is sometimes overlooked, it is worth scrutinising for the sheer perfection of its design. This very heavy hat block was the perfect vessel for anchoring these flighty orchids.'

SEAN COOK

STEP ONE
I used a low aluminium hat block, but a low, wide (about 30 centimetre diameter) white salad bowl or ceramic bowl would also work; don't use a transparent vessel as you want to disguise the floral foam. Place a piece of wet floral foam in the centre, to anchor the flowers.

STEP TWO
Divide six stems of phalaenopsis orchids into two clusters (containing three stems each), then place stems in water vials; orchids last longer placed in water vials rather than directly into soaked floral foam.

STEP THREE
Push one cluster of orchids into each side of the floral foam, leaving a gap between them. Place 3–5 large unusual *Alocasia amazonica* leaves in the central gap so that they cascade down and over the edge of the vessel.

Aluminium hat block, 19th-century French marble butcher's block and 19th-century French arched-top windows from The Country Trader.

STEP ONE
The kales here have a short, stubby stem and being the larger, heavier element, I put them to the front right-hand side of the vase first to give the arrangement a supportive base.

STEP TWO
Next, I added two branches of twisted filbert or witch hazel (cut to 1.5 metres) on either side, towards the back of the vase, giving the arrangement structure and shape.

STEP THREE
I placed two long stems of cymbidium orchids in the centre as the hero flowers, while the 3–5 shorter and more delicate stems of phalaenopsis and cattleya orchids were woven in amongst the kale.

This piece of background fabric from Collette Dinnigan was the inspiration for this arrangement. The detail of the design is quite baroque and initially it made me think of a twisted filbert or witch hazel (*Corylus avellana* 'Contorta') branch, with its gold dripping catkins. Kale is so frilly-looking, it's almost like a fabric, while orchids have that rich, delicate decadence. As always, the container has its own important part to play. We found this Murano vase at The Country Trader and thought the gold running through it would work well against the fabric. This is a good example of using a vase that is quite tall without needing to have stems that reach all the way down to the bottom.

This is quite a long-lasting arrangement, but kale, a cabbage relative, can get a bit smelly, so it's good to put a capful of bleach into the water. Every three days, change the water, adding a capful of bleach each time.

Murano glass vase from The Country Trader.
19th-century Dutch chest of drawers. Printed silk voile fabric courtesy of Collette Dinnigan.

'As well as being beautiful, this Madagascar orchid has an intriguing background. Although today it is known by its botanical name, *Angraecum sesquipedale*, many years ago it was given such names as "vegetable starfish", "comet orchid", "Star of Bethlehem orchid", and "rocket orchid", but it certainly lives up to its true title of "King of the Angraecums".

Angraecum sesquipedale grows indigenously in the hot lowlands of the east coast of Madagascar and Saint-Marie Islands. In 1822 the famous French explorer and botanist Aubert-Aubert du Petit Thouars first named this orchid species *Angraecum sesquipedale*, which, when translated from the Latin literally means "measuring a foot and a half"; and when the flower is measured from top to bottom, it certainly approaches this length!

It was not until 1854 that *Angraecum sesquipedale* was first introduced into European greenhouses by the Englishman Rev. William Ellis. In 1862, Charles Darwin proposed that there must be a nocturnal hawkmoth in Madagascar with a sufficiently long tongue (proboscis) to reach the nectar in the flower's 30–33 centimetre spur. He was ridiculed for this suggestion, but as he predicted, this moth, *Xanthopan morgani praedicta*, was eventually discovered, but not until some 40 years later.

Although I grow numerous Madagascan orchids and have learnt much regarding their history from reading *An Introduction to the Cultivated Angraecoid Orchids of Madagascar*, by Fred Hillerman and Arthur Holst (Timber Press), *Angraecum sesquipedale* holds an unfailing fascination for me and is definitely the pride of my collection.'

GOWAN STEWART

Gowan Stewart, of Wirra Willa Orchids, has always been an inspiration, with her knowledge and total passion for what she does. She is completely immersed in her love of rare and beautiful orchids and other plants – and helps make our job simple.

STEP ONE
Three lovingly cultivated Madagascar (*Angraecum sesquipedale*) orchid plants were placed in pots on a table.

STEP TWO
Moss was then wrapped around the pots and secured with leather thonging.

STEP THREE
Gowan added extra roots at the front of the pots for effect.

19th-century French painted doors and limed oak 1940s table (one of a pair) from Howell and Howell.

'Violets. So Victorian, so perfect. Violets and cut crystal are classic.'

KIRSTIE CLEMENTS

STEP ONE

Keep approximately 50 violets grouped together in six posies, with their leaves forming a border of green around the flowers. Tie off each posy with a piece of twine.

STEP TWO

Place the posies in a crystal bowl filled almost to the top with water, layering the posies so they sit at differing heights. To do this, start by placing three posies around the edge of the bowl, then add the remaining posies, working towards the centre. Take care not to form a perfect ball, rather try to keep the posies at slightly irregular heights.

STEP THREE

As violets like to drink from their petals, spray the flower blooms each day with a mister to keep them fresh. Or sink them upside-down in water to revive for 30 minutes, then return them to the vase. Violets have a wonderful, old-fashioned charm and fragrance.

Waterford crystal bowl.

'Flowers in full bloom: bountiful, cascading and perfumed, evoking memories. Inviting you to fall into them and smile as you pass by.'

ELEONORA TRIGUBOFF

Eleonora loves her flowers to be loose and very abundant and luxurious. This magnolia arrangement stands about 1.5 metres high. I needed the three containers to keep its wayward appeal; I wanted it to look as if it were still growing.

STEP ONE
I used 5–6 large stems of magnolia. Starting at the back with the tallest stems, I tilted them against the side of the oil jars.

STEP TWO
I then worked the finer, smaller branches in amongst the larger ones, making sure I placed a few leaning towards the front. This made it possible to look into some blooms at eye level.

STEP ONE
Strip three 50–60 centimetre-high gum nut stems of their leaves, then place them in a tall vase half-filled with water.

STEP TWO
Cut three cymbidium orchid stems to approximately 40 centimetre lengths, then push them in between the gum nut stems to anchor the gum stems in a more upright position. I wanted it to look as though the gum nuts were almost dancing across the tops of the orchids.

STEP THREE
Place an alocasia 'Green Velvet' and an *Anthurium warocqueanum* leaf behind the orchid flowers to pose as the orchid's leaf.

I wanted to create a strong, almost Australian-safari appearance against the background of this rough kilim wall hanging. Here, these unusual cymbidium orchids are almost unrecognisable. They produce a wonderful fleshy texture and give the gum nuts room to exhibit their sculptural forms; without the orchids, the gum branches wouldn't have as much power. It was important to cut the orchid stems short and cluster them to the front of the vase in order to see all their faces pushed together in a group. To me, this is a very masculine arrangement and, fittingly, it was placed in a gentleman's cigar room. The white textural vase adds an extra dimension of strength.

David Edmonds 'carved vase' in vanilla from Macleay on Manning. Kilim wall hanging. *Vogue Living* penthouse, Sydney.

'My childhood memory of japonica is of walking through the Kyoto streets in the chilly winter air. When I saw their blossoms, sometimes even with snow resting on them, I felt filled with emotional warmth as I realised that spring was just around the corner.'

AKIRA ISOGAWA

STEP ONE
Take four bunches (approximately twelve stems) of japonica or flowering quince, then separate each branch, laying each one on the ground or on a table.

STEP TWO
Taking time to observe each branch to note its individual form, cut one of the larger pieces into an approximately 1 metre length, then place it on an angle in a tall vase.

STEP THREE
Repeat with a similar-sized branch using a second vase.

STEP FOUR
Weave the remaining branches between the two initial branches, taking care not to build them up too fully or the unique shape and line of each branch will be spoilt. Most of the other branches should follow the placement and line of the initial two.

Peony print tulle fabric courtesy of Akira Isogawa. Table and pair of Chinese Mandarin umbrella stands, Qing Dynasty (1644–1911), from Lynette Cunnington Chinese Art and Furniture.

spring

in season

september

allium, *Banksia praemorsa*, boronia, bluebell, blushing bride, cherry blossom, cyclamen, *Eucalyptus youngiana*, flannel flower, freesia, Geraldton wax, gymea lily, isopogon, hippeastrum, hyacinth (including grape hyacinth), japonica (flowering quince), jasmine, lily-of-the-valley, orchids, rhododendron, sweet pea, tulip, waratah (pink, red and white)

october

arum lily (especially 'Pink Marshmallow'), *Banksia baxteri* (cones), *Banksia praemorsa*, bearded iris, cyclamen, dogwood, *Eucalyptus macrocarpa*, freesia, garden roses, guelder rose, gymea lily, hippeastrum, isopogon, lilac, lily-of-the-valley

november

Banksia praemorsa, bearded iris, bromeliad, calla lily, dogwood, hydrangea, leucadendron (seed pods), lilium (especially November lily), roses (including 'Bianca', 'Baccara' and 'Julia's Rose'), pink waratah

also in spring

allium, amaryllis, arum lily, azalea, boronia, calceolaria, daffodil, delphinium, freesia, lisianthus, misty blue (limonium), paper daisy, peony, poppies, Queen Anne's lace, ranunculus, sarracenia, succulents, sunflower, sweet pea, waratah, waterlily, zinnia

Margaret supplied us with an amazing portfolio she had compiled over the years of all sorts of floral inspirations. There were countless pictures of gardens and vase arrangements Margaret had assiduously collected from Australia and overseas. We, in turn, used this as our inspiration for creating this piece.

STEP ONE

The larger arrangement to the right was made by starting off with a base of approximately five stems of white hydrangea and two groups of David Austin roses, which I placed towards the front of the vessel.

STEP TWO

I then added three small bunches of hellebores in the pockets between the hydrangeas, thereby creating a good base for randomly slotting in ten white-tipped tulips.

STEP THREE

I placed two David Austin roses, one to the front, the other to the right, as bold accents of colour. I then added a single stunning stem of rhododendron.

STEP FOUR

The last touch was nestling a smaller vase containing a striking bunch of trimmed strawberry-coloured 'Double Delight' roses to the left of the larger key arrangement.

'In his essay *De Profundis*, Oscar Wilde said, "flowers are part of desire." I can't imagine a world without them; if it was a toss-up between a meal and a bunch of roses, I'd take the roses.'

MARGARET FINK

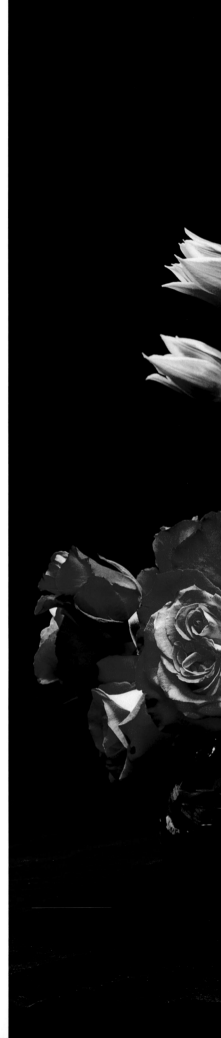

STEP ONE

When working with urns, it is best to fill them with an appropriately sized bucket, then to top the bucket with floral foam. This helps to give the form and shape an arrangement in an urn often needs.

STEP TWO

For the background I pushed ten stems of smoke bush (*Cotinus coggygria*) foliage, cut into various lengths, into the floral foam, to form a starfish-shape.

STEP THREE

Next I layered approximately five hosta leaves at the front of the urn, then added some bear grass (*Xerophyllum*) and nestled two bunches of 'Julia's Rose' down low against the leaves.

STEP FOUR

As a final touch, I added the accent flowers intermittently throughout the arrangement, including a few flannel flowers and rhododendrons, a little pompom bush (*Verticordia*) and drumsticks (*Isopogon drummondii*).

'Travelling is an exotic adventure. Remember the first time you walked into a really grand hotel and there was the most enormous, astonishing floral arrangement that made the whole place, and everyone in it, look so elegant and chic?'

PAMELA EASTON AND LYDIA PEARSON

19th-century cast-iron ornamental fountain. Martyn Cook Antiques.

Bear in mind that dogwood (*Cornus kousa*)
branches usually flower along one surface.
Take an individual stem of dogwood
(approximately 1 metre long) and place
it in a large vase, using a rock to anchor
the stem in position so the flowers are
displayed as a blanket across the top of the
leaves. If tipped the wrong way, the flowers
can look as though they are hanging upside
down on the branch.

One day I wish to go to the dogwood forests in America.
The first time I saw the dogwood tree's lustrous flowers,
I couldn't believe the way they spread themselves across
the top of the branch. I always wonder why such a
beautiful flower has such a hard-sounding, solid name.
The fact that its name is not as lyrical as those of many
other flowers makes it even more fascinating and
appealing to me.

It's hard to make an arrangement with dogwood.
It's always a wrestling match to wrangle it — its branches
never sit quite right in the vase to showcase the correct
direction of the flowers. They have an unpredictable
longevity and are at their best placed in a vase alone,
without other flowers.

Japanese floral fabric by Florence
Broadhurst, courtesy of Signature Prints.

Hippeastrums are wonderful when you place them in a vase, tight in bud and watch them open up against each other. With all the petals overlapping and interlocking, they seem like a closely-knit family. They also have wonderful, fleshy, hollow stems and I love the sound of cutting them. When you look deep into the flower you can often see the most intense lime-green colour. I always feel like I could just fall in there and be enveloped forever. Each petal has a very shimmery crystal quality when scrutinised closely.

Hippeastrums can also be very beautiful as a plant in pots placed along the middle of a table. People will often buy ten potted bulbs wrapped in our architectural tracing paper, and then line them up and down their dining table for a relaxed, informal and inexpensive centrepiece.

When working with hippeastrums, take care not to crush the open flowers. In fact, I would advise you not to even lay them down on a table, as even this can bruise the delicate flowers. Instead, keep them upright in a bucket while preparing your arrangement.

STEP ONE
Starting with four bunches of hippeastrums, bundle the stems together firmly in your hand, taking care not to crush the fragile stems.

STEP TWO
Cut the stems on a sharp angle, then place the cluster of hippeastrums in the opening of the vase in one large group. It is ideal to place the flowers in the vase while they are still in bud, allowing them to open up in their arranged position.

'Bird in Paradise' vase by Christian Tortu from Macleay on Manning. 'Spring floral' by Florence Broadhurst, courtesy of Signature Prints.

STEP ONE
Quarter-fill a large, heavy vase with water. It is advisable to create the arrangement on the surface you wish to display it. Stand a group of 4–5 rolled banana trunk husks upright in the vase, then fan them out slightly towards the right side.

STEP TWO
Insert a large, strong palm husk into the vase, placing it on a severe angle to the left-hand side. Lay a trimmed branch of sword lily *(Doryanthes palmeri)* along the centre of this strong husk. Add a few dark red cordyline leaves to the back of the arrangement, to either side of the banana husk.

STEP THREE
Lay another branch of sword lily on the table, lengthways in front of the vase, then top it with another strong palm husk, so that it rests upon the left-hand side of the sword lily.

'Food and flowers have a lot in common and can truly complement one another. They share colour, texture, vibrancy, aroma and even flavour. Both are affected by the seasons and temperatures. I believe that the two go together, hand-in-hand, to help create a great atmosphere and elevate the senses in my restaurant. At ARIA, we enjoy having stunning floral arrangements that suit the restaurant décor, as well as our fine food. Grandiflora always provide us with the most beautiful flowers; they bring the room to life without taking too much away from the restaurant environment.'

MATT MORAN

ARIA Restaurant, Sydney.

STEP ONE

The beauty of this arrangement lies
in its seeming simplicity. I first lined a
Waterford crystal vase with a bed of moss.
I then placed a very large and particularly
spectacular phalaenopsis orchid plant in
its pot onto the bed of moss in the vase.

STEP TWO

In the foreground, I lined a low cube vase
with a bed of moss, then placed another
shorter, more curved phalaenopsis orchid
plant (with its soil attached and in its pot)
inside the vase, sitting in the moss.

STEP THREE

I then placed a stem of phalaenopsis
orchid (cut into a 40 centimetre length)
into a water vial and pushed the vial
into the soil of the small cube vase.

'To me, an orchid is just like love: strong, beautiful and uniquely individual, yet so, so fragile.'

PETER MORRISSEY

Waterford crystal vase in background. Peter
Morrissey's own square vase in foreground.
Apartment of Peter Morrissey.

First, trim the stems of two individual Honolulu lilies, one to 40 centimetres and the other to 25 centimetres.

STEP TWO
Place them in a vase. I used a vase with a narrow neck to support the short stems of the lilies and hold the flowers upright.

STEP THREE
I then placed a circular piece of glass at the front of the vase. Its function is purely decorative, and it is placed there to encourage interest by introducing another shape, colour and form to the composition. Don't be afraid to add extra objects to stimulate both the eye and the imagination.

The Honolulu lily (*Solandra maxima*) has to be up there with my top-five favourite flowers. In bud, it couldn't be more sensual; when it opens, it makes the mind boggle. I love observing the venation inside the lily and the exquisite movement of its stamens; then to top it all off, when you're looking at it that closely, a waft of its fragrance is overpowering in a most summery way. This lily has a wonderful thick vine with luscious green leaves and is a fast grower; unfortunately, it doesn't last long as a cut flower.

Vase and 17th-century northern Italian Cloud Mirror from The Country Trader. Circular glass piece in foreground from Object Gallery. *Vogue Living* penthouse, Sydney.

This arrangement was built around the romantic atmosphere of Queen Anne's lace. The 'Dolce Vita' and 'Spirit of Peace' roses seemed perfect choices for such an old-fashioned combination.

I imagine this bunch of flowers being gathered directly from somebody's garden, with the allium, hydrangea, hippeastrum, roses and copper beech all being plucked straight from their plants. I can see it lying in the arms of the lady of the house as she strolls through the garden with wind-swept hair, *Wuthering Heights*-style.

STEP ONE
Fill a round, low glass vase three-quarters with water. Cut the stems of two bunches (10 stems) of large-headed, pale white-pink hydrangeas to 20 centimetres, then pull the elastic bands up to the base of the flowers. Place one bunch on each side of the vase.

STEP TWO
Take two bunches of 'Dolce Vita' roses andtie them with green cord halfway up their stems. Place them in the arrangement, slightly off centre. It is important not to see elastic bands in an arrangement, so when in doubt, substitute them with ribbon, cord, tie or thonging.

STEP THREE
Add ten stems of 'Spirit of Peace' roses in between these two clusters. Insert two bunches of seeded Queen Anne's lace, one on either side of the 'Dolce Vita' roses.

STEP FOUR
Place two stems of hippeastrums (cut to 35 centimetres) to the top left-hand side of the arrangement, between the roses. Nestle the hippeastrums amongst the roses to create a great open shape towards the centre when they burst open.

STEP FIVE
Add one bunch (10 stems) of allium flowers to the back. Insert 3–4 wispy branches of copper beech to the right-hand side of the vase, trailing down as a final flourish.

Sarracenia flowers, also known as pitcher plants, are an extremely specialised tropical flower. They're quite an expensive little flower, and not to everyone's taste. I like the way this fly-catcher flower looks like a parachute, with its funny bulbous centre and petals. Grouped together here, their lime-green colour is a wonderful clash against the tomato-red of the Japanese Washi paper we've used as a background. I also like how the round pattern of the sarracenia centres is replicated in the wallpaper pattern, as well as in the circles formed by this extraordinary specimen vase by Christian Tortu.

Sarracenia flowers also grow in burgundy, and I've used a few of these here to create an interesting shadow effect, almost allowing the lime-green colour to jump forward. There are quite a lot of flowers for this vase, but I think it works. We have never been given sarracenia flowers with their leaves intact, so I cross-hatched their thin stems to anchor them. They're a nice way to start spring, which is when sarracenia flowers are in season.

STEP ONE
Start with seven sarracenia flowers. Place the longer stemmed flowers into the vase first, then individually cut the remaining flowers down to the desired lengths as you place them.

STEP TWO
Remembering the rule of grouping flowers in clusters of either three or five stems, place three of the green sarracenias on the left-hand side of the vase and five leaning towards the right-hand side. Add a few burgundy sarracenias to the back of the vase, towards the left, and to the front of the vase, towards the right.

STEP THREE
Cut down a tropical alocasia leaf, then place at the front of the vase. Angle a second alocasia leaf out to the right-hand side of the vase.

Vase by Christian Tortu.

I find the purity of this elegant vase of
'Bianca' roses very alluring and the pebbles
make it very Tetsuya. These exquisite roses
were collected from one of our suppliers,
Lorna and Barry Osborne, who grew them
in their garden.

STEP ONE

Start by trimming 4–5 bunches of roses
completely of their foliage and cutting their
stems to 30–40 centimetre lengths. Group
them into bundles of ten stems, then join
them together as one large group.

STEP TWO

Place the stems into a cube vase, then
rearrange by shifting the roses, pulling
them up to various heights.

STEP THREE

A few extra stems may need to be cut
short (15–20 centimetres) and occasionally
added throughout the arrangement,
pushed in low. Others may need to be left
long (30–40 centimetres), then interspersed
throughout the arrangement.

STEP FOUR

It is important to have undulation, where
some roses are placed to recess and others
placed to protrude, as this gives an uneven
appeal to the arrangement.

'I love the white rose for its simplicity — either a single rose or a large bunch.'

TETSUYA WAKUDA

Batik fabric handmade by
Shumei Kobayashi in background.
Tetsuya's Restaurant, Sydney.

'Lily-of-the-valley was always Christian Dior's flower. I believe he had them to the right of his desk every day of his working life. It became his symbol, which he sewed into the linings of his couture gowns; I always thought that was quite special.

Georgia O'Keefe was one of the first painters to inspire me as I was growing up and my mum's art books were always a point of reference. In her paintings, flowers became dissected landscapes, their shapes reflective of human forms. I love the incongruity of roses and bones. It is this spirit that I enjoy in design.

I write this with a bunch of gardenias to the left of my table from a friend's garden; simple gestures bring so much happiness. My partner Jason has a madcap way of arranging flowers that seems to baffle most florists. He combines the oddest collections of flowers, yet they seem to work so magically. It is such a good reflection of him; always thinking outside the boundaries. It reminds me of what the creative is all about and seems such an honest window to the heart.'

MICHELLE JANK

This arrangement is pure inspiration. What makes it so magical is the notion of simply going into a garden or market and grabbing a few flowers, then randomly popping them into vases. You can have just as beautiful an impact with a few flowers and get a lot of enjoyment out of one individual flower developing over a week. I also like the way that it's not always just about flowers facing forwards and being obvious; this reflects the way things grow in nature.

STEP ONE
This sort of spontaneous arrangement involves being a bit playful and not being too safe. Michelle used an assortment of bottles and flowers, including poppies, peonies and lily-of-the-valley: some of the stems were kept long, while some were trimmed short, and others were still just a bud.

STEP TWO
It also provides an opportunity to consider using different containers: jars, teapots, teacups, ceramics and even modern glass bottles are all worthy vessels. Mostly, it's about being open to whatever triggers your eye as you go through your day, and then having fun with it.

Assorted bottles from davidmetnicole.

STEP ONE
Starting with four small Christian Tortu
vases (although any beautiful, simple,
small vases would do), I collected
2–3 hippeastrum blooms per vase,
depending on the size of each vase neck.

STEP TWO
I then cut the stems to the height of each
vase and placed two or three in each vessel
so their blooms interlocked, taking care
that they didn't hang unbecomingly down
over the edge of the vases and look lifeless.

Working in front of such a strong artwork by Marion Borgelt,
I felt it was important to keep the blooms and vessels simple.
The vase shape is reminiscent of hippeastrums when they go
to pod. White hippeastrums signify complete purity to me.
Clean, crisp and elegant, they are a beautiful wedding flower.

'Egg' vases by Christian Tortu.
Artwork by Marion Borgelt,
Liquid Light: No. 23, 2004 (Detail).
Vogue Living penthouse, Sydney.

STEP ONE

I used a low round glass vase (approximately 20 centimetres tall) and placed four stems of pink rhododendron around the rim. I then added one bunch of gardenias (approximately five stems) to the left of the vase, building the arrangement up with kalmia flowers, but you could use luculia instead.

STEP TWO

Next, I poked 'Angel Face' roses in groups of threes to each side and towards the top of the arrangement, helping to build up the height.

STEP THREE

In the final stages, I added two stems of pale pink phalaenopsis orchids, making sure the flowers were pulled around to the front to show their faces.

STEP FOUR

Going back over the arrangement, I placed one or two individual blooms such as gardenias or roses, making the bouquet more mixed and light.

'My love of flowers comes from my darling mother. Her garden is full of old-fashioned things: dahlias; hydrangeas; camellias; port wine magnolia; highly scented rhododendron; freesias; jasmine; roses; November lilies; an ancient lemon tree; various fruit trees; and vegetables. As early as I can remember, Mum would place a tiny cut-glass vase full of sweet little things in my bedroom; often 'Cécile Brünner' roses, which she calls 'sweetheart roses'. She still does this whenever I go home; a little vase full of love.'

MAY LLOYD

'The purple iris gives me great joy. From my childhood,
I can see my mother arranging a generous bunch of irises
in a big creamy white vase and the effect of their unusual
colour and supple form evoked the romantic within me.'

DAMIEN PIGNOLET

I have tried here to replicate the beauty of
the iris in its most natural state, as it would
grow in a garden. I did not clean away any
dead bud husks from the stems. I also
used apricot iris, interspersed with the
purple iris; the colour of the apricot iris is so
pale and translucent, like peachy skin.

STEP ONE
Take care not to damage these delicate
flowers; it is best to lay them on a table
or bench with the flower heads hanging
over the edge.

STEP TWO
Remove any broken flowers, remembering
that new buds will appear when the old
flowers have been removed. Trim the
stems to 50–60 centimetre lengths.

STEP THREE
Half-fill two trough vases with water,
then fill both vases with approximately
six bunches of irises (about 30 stems
in each vase).

STEP FOUR
Place another 15 stems unevenly between
the two vases, to add a variety of heights
and create a more natural effect.

Glass trough vases. English George IV
(c.1830) mahogany demi-lune sideboard
from Martyn Cook Antiques.

STEP ONE
Four orchids were trimmed short,
then gently placed on their sides,
resting on the rim of a crystal factice.

'These very rare *Masdevallia × falcata* orchids were graciously supplied by one of our orchid growers. When we received this box of orchid specimens at the Flower Markets, we knew we had to use them but weren't quite sure how, as they are such a delicate, small flower. I then fortuitously spied this amazing cut-crystal factice which had the sun streaming through it. This is a totally impractical arrangement as the flowers are merely sitting on top of the crystal. When cut, they only last for a few days in water, so laying the flowers across the crystal highlighted this fragility and the orchids' truly ephemeral nature.'

SEAN COOK

Factice from The Country Trader.
Vogue Living penthouse, Sydney.

STEP ONE
First I put a container inside a large stone trough, which we do with vessels that could be damaged or leak if directly filled with water.

STEP TWO
I then cut five bromeliad plants from their pots and placed them in the trough in two groups at right angles to each other, one facing the front of the container, the other facing the left-hand side. The bromeliads are the element which gives this arrangement its structure.

STEP THREE
Next, I pushed one bunch of gum nuts down low, to the front left-hand side of the container.

STEP FOUR
I then cut three bunches of 'Pink Marshmallow' arum lilies to 40 centimetre lengths and slipped them down in between the bromeliad plants, to the right of the gum nuts.

Recently introduced to us at Grandiflora, this 'Pink Marshmallow' arum lily has won our hearts. Its fleshy nude-pink colour stains the inner part of the flower and stamen; each flower looks hand-dyed. Massed together, they look incredible in a simple glass vase.

Unusually, here I cut them down low and nestled them amongst these bromeliads in order to be able to look down into the flowers. We have coined these arum lillies as the signature flower for one of Australia's leading designers, Iain Halliday — he imagines them in his alabaster urn. Every Friday during the warmer months, we keep an armful of them aside for his regular house flowers.

Balinese stone trough. Red bamboo screen.
Antler stone bowl by Mitchell English.

Dedicated to my mother, Louise, my flower muse and greatest critic, there's an old-fashioned quality to this combination. With a cloud of gossamer floating across the background, it strikes me as being ethereal. Something about it reminds me of the 1920s era – of flappers and ladies with feathers in their hair, wearing them to the side. The black centres of the anemones catch the eye like little buttons or jewels placed in amongst the flowers, and the pieris, or lily-of-the-valley shrub (*Pieris forrestii*), always has a wonderful tasselly effect. This arrangement is textural and sumptuous and has an antique quality; I can imagine it in a stately old wood-panelled parlour with ladies sitting around taking high tea.

STEP ONE
Take three bunches of guelder roses (*Viburnum opulus*) and cut the stems to approximately 60 centimetre lengths, then trim the foliage if it is torn or marked. Lean bunches at right angles to each other, splaying out from a low, wide, round vase.

STEP TWO
Cut two bunches of pieris to similar lengths, then place them around and next to the guelder rose bunches. Take 3–5 stems of large, dark green philodendron leaves (*Philodendron* 'Emerald Green') and push them under the cluster of pieris at the base and to the left of the arrangement.

STEP THREE
Feed in three bunches of anemone flowers, then add ten individual cream roses which have been stripped of thorns, in groups of either three or five throughout the arrangement.

STEP FOUR
Finally, add one delicate stem of phalaenopsis orchid towards the centre of the arrangement.

Background Blinds by Bayliss.

122

STEP ONE
Place a piece of floral foam in a bowl-shaped vase or container, leaving gaps down each side. Add some water. Using three bunches of hippeastrums cut to 30–35 centimetre lengths, firmly place hippeastrum stems in two groups, one on either side of the floral foam. It is hard to push these stems into floral foam; this is why I opt for putting them in the gaps leaning between the floral foam and vase, and resting directly in fresh water.

STEP TWO
To form the flower base, working in bunches of five stems, feed approximately three bunches of peonies, cut to 25–35 centimetre lengths, into the floral foam and down the side of the vase.

STEP THREE
Take three individual peony blooms and slot them in over the top of the flower base so that they sit higher and are more protruding than the other flowers. The idea is to create some unevenness so that the arrangement doesn't look like a perfect dome.

The peony has a feathery appearance, which reminds me of the softness and shape of a dove's breast; the challenge here was to capture the idea of that sensation. These peonies are very open and full-blown. I feel like I could run my hands across the flowers, close my eyes, and believe I was stroking a dove. Including the hippeastrums gives the arrangement a contrasting shape. The hippeastrum flowers create a division down the centre of the peonies. As both flowers are similar in colour, it almost seems as though the hippeastrums could be mutated peonies.

Silver bowl from Cavit and Co. Pty Ltd.
Acid-etched black wallpaper by Ilias.
Vogue Living penthouse, Sydney.

This inspirational combination of sandstone and native flowers is quite abstract in its construction. A low cube vase filled with water sits between and behind the pieces of sandstone.

STEP TWO
Four waratahs with their foliage intact were placed into the vase at varying heights. Another waratah sits at the base of the arrangement; I hid it between the rocks with its stem in a water vial. You can also wrap water vials in leaves to disguise them throughout the arrangement.

STEP THREE
I then trimmed the ends of three large bunches (30 stems) of flannel flowers to 45 centimetre lengths and cleared them of most of their foliage. They were placed in the vase to sit in a group high above the waratahs. A few shorter stems were placed behind the waratahs to the left-hand side.

'Perched up high in the Blue Mountains is our piece of paradise, where an edible garden meets the bush. The sprays of flannel flowers and waratahs that loosely frame our patch are not only striking with their torch-like vibrancy and contrasting foliage, but are a poignant testament to camaraderie and resilience in nature.'

SEAN MORAN

For my part, roses in Vivienne Sharpe's apartment against this painting by Tim Maguire were a must-do. This is my favourite painting in the world and we couldn't give Vivienne anything but roses. She comes into the shop all the time, determined to find particular garden roses which one of our suppliers grows along his driveway.

There's a wonderful opulence in putting flowers against a backdrop such as a painting and displaying them on a reflective surface; the surroundings become part of the arrangement. While I mostly used glass vessels here, we loved the reflection of the single gold vase in the table; it really gives balance to the arrangement. There was much workshopping over the space between each vase. We initially pushed them very close together, but in the end decided they needed breathing space between them to accommodate the stunning background. A lot of these flowers have marked or not-quite-perfect petals, which to me is part of their beauty.

STEP ONE

Strip approximately 15 bunches (150 stems) of garden roses of most of their foliage and thorns, to about half-way up their stems.

STEP TWO

Using approximately 50 stems, create a big bunch of roses, shaping them in your hand (pulling some up and pushing some down) until you have what looks like a lovely bunch. Bear in mind the distribution of colour in the arrangement.

STEP THREE

Cut the stems on an angle so that they are level. Using a selection of five differently sized vases, place this bunch into the biggest vase. Building on this base, poke in individual blooms and more hero blooms, to add splashes of colour and varying shapes.

STEP FOUR

Create smaller bunches for the remaining vases, then pick one or two stems from the original vase to add as a highlight, or to use if a particular colour, shape, or more open or closed rose is needed.

'These are my birthday roses, my Christmas roses, my good-to-be-alive roses. I love the fragrance and the colours. Both classic and contemporary, they are simply irresistible.'

VIVIENNE SHARPE

Painting by Tim Maguire.
Apartment of Vivienne Sharpe.

The simplicity of this shot was inspired by the quiet tranquillity of this Louhan Torso sandstone sculpture (12th-century, Sichuan Province, China). Flowers don't always need to be displayed in vases. In many different cultures and countries, flowers are threaded, floated, scattered or pinned rather than always placed upright in a vase. It is refreshing to think outside of the square and push the boundaries with new ideas. Being brave plays an important role in forcing out creative ideas.

Flowers for a party (one night) are often okay if they don't have an abundant water supply (naturally, depending on the type of flower) and this can give more flexibility with creative ideas. Keeping flowers looking good for long periods is always challenging — this is where using a water vial allows for greater freedom.

STEP ONE
Simply draping two stems of phalaenopsis orchids across the sculpture's lower niche provided a dramatic contrast of softness against the coarseness of the stone.

STEP TWO
By containing the stems in individual water vials, this installation can last for several weeks if you change the water and re-cut the stems every two or three days.

12th-century Louhan Torso sandstone sculpture, Sichuan Province, China. Home of Iain Halliday.

STEP ONE

Cut a bunch (2–3 stems) of gum to a length of 50 centimetres. Keep the leaves at the top still attached. Nestle the lower part of the branch with the gum nuts attached to the left against the neck of a large, wide-necked vase.

STEP TWO

Cut three white waratahs ('Wirreanda White') to various lengths, stripping the leaves at the base of the stems but leaving the foliage intact closer to the flowers, as the leaves have a wonderful shape. Push them into the vase, next to the gum branch, which forms the basis of the arrangement.

STEP THREE

As a final touch, feed in 5–6 kangaroo paws throughout the gum stems and to the right of the vase, amongst the waratahs.

The amazing painted Chinese screen in the background was the perfect inspiration for using these bold native flowers. The greens are so subtle and the rare white waratah, when placed alongside the dusty green kangaroo paw and gum, is an unusual choice. Here, the handmade vase by Alexia Gnecchi Ruscone is visually just as important as the blooms.

This arrangement is a fusion of Australia (Alexia's modern vase, combined with the waratahs and gum) and Asia (the old-world screen purchased by Paulo Gnecchi Ruscone in China).

Vase handmade by Alexia Gnecchi Ruscone.
Home of Alexia and Paulo Gnecchi Ruscone.

Anyone who has a good sense of design gets excited when we use streamlined glass trough vases in our arrangements. The thing I like best about these vases is that they can make the flowers look like they are suspended. Bulbs work especially well with their flowers attached and blooming: you can have a row of tulips, amaryllis, or anything really.

I love how luxurious the black calla lilies look against the medusa leaves (*Anthurium* 'Medusa'). The vessel disappears, leaving them to float on their own. It's easy to form good shapes in such a long and narrow vase because you can easily wedge flowers very firmly into it.

This arrangement is very long-lasting. The leaves last around six weeks and the black calla lilies, in season from winter right through to early summer, are hardy and long-lasting too.

You could place this arrangement on a bar or window ledge. We have also used this arrangement as the table centrepiece for weddings and product launches.

STEP ONE
This arrangement required a bit of concentration. I rolled groups of approximately 3–5 medusa leaves around my hand to form two coils. I then pushed the coils, one at a time, into a glass trough vase three-quarters filled with water, holding them down to see whether any of the coils would unfurl. I placed the first coil against one end of the vase, then placed another coil next to it.

STEP TWO
I arranged two bunches of calla lilies separately in my hand, making one bigger than the other, then cut the stems so the flowers hovered above the edge of the vase.

STEP THREE
Separating two coils of medusa leaves with my hands, I wedged the large bunch of calla lilies in a tight cluster at one end of the vase, then wedged the smaller bunch at the opposite end of another trough vase. I pulled a few lilies a little higher to give them a feeling of movement.

STEP FOUR
I draped a few leaves over the front right-hand edge of the front vase – it's important to have a few leaves coming out of the vase, as the arrangement would look too contrived if they were all wrapped in tight coils. I felt that it needed the contrast between the tight coils and the release of the looser leaves.

134

summer

in season

d e c e m b e r agapanthus, allium, amaranthus, amaryllis, *Banksia attenuata*, *Banksia menziesii* (seed pods), berzilia, buddleia, calla lily, celosia, chestnut, Christmas bell, Christmas bush, dahlia, *Eucalyptus ficifolia*, frangipani, gardenias (including 'Florida', 'Magnifica' and 'Professor Pucci') hydrangea, leucodendron (seed pods), lilium (including oriental and November lily), peony, roses (including 'Brother Cadfael', 'Cool Water', 'Enchantment', 'Mary Webb', 'Sahara', 'Spirit of Peace' and 'Valencia'), smoke bush, stephanotis

j a n u a r y agapanthus, amaryllis, beehive ginger, berzilia, bouvardia, calla lily, celosia, copper beech, crabapple, *Curcuma alismatifolia* (also sold as Siam tulip), dahlia, figs on branches, flowering ginger, flowering gum, frangipani, gardenias (including 'Florida', 'Magnifica' and 'Professor Pucci'), gloriosa lily (*Gloriosa* 'Rothschildiana'), hydrangea (green), lotus (flowers and seed pods), roses (especially 'Bianca', 'Birmingham Post', 'Brandy', 'Candy', 'Cécile Brünner', 'Cleopatra', David Austin roses, 'Fragrant Cloud', 'Just Joey', 'Mr Lincoln' and garden roses), nepenthes (pitcher plants), stephanotis

f e b r u a r y alpinia ginger, artemisia, bouvardia, *Curcuma alismatifolia* (also sold as Siam tulip), dahlia, gardenia, hydrangea (green and *H. paniculata*), lilium (especially Casablanca lily and *Lilium regale*), lotus (flowers and seed pods), roses (especially 'Camp David', David Austin roses, 'Elina', 'Julia's Rose', 'Pretty Jessica' and 'Winchester Cathedral'), tuberose, waterlily

a l s o i n s u m m e r arum lily (*Zantedeschia aethiopica*), succulents

STEP ONE
Start by building groups of five cream arum
lilies (*Zantedeschia aethiopica*) into a good
handful, then place them in your vessel; in
this case, I used Iain's urn. At Grandiflora
we often put a container into receptacles
(such as this) that could be damaged or
leak if filled directly with water.

STEP TWO
Working in bunches, add extra cream arum
lilies whose stems have been kept slightly
longer than those of the initial group, to
build up height to the back and left-hand
side of the arrangement. This arrangement
has excellent longevity.

'I'm not one to wax lyrical about flowers. All I know is that to me, a domestic interior
is incomplete without beautiful flowers, and the best flowers I know come from
Grandiflora. If you are lucky enough to receive Saskia Havekes' flowers, they never
disappoint. Every other florist in Australia is like a compromise.'

IAIN HALLIDAY

This arrangement reminds me of a hot Sydney summer's day. Figs on branches often feature in our summer arrangements, along with liliums and beautiful, luxurious tropical leaves. The curls of the nepenthes plant are what I found most attractive and exciting to work with here. Often pushing stems against their natural direction can produce an interesting shape in an arrangement. I particularly liked the lime-green quality of all these liliums (also sold as Casablanca lilies) in bud. Even though my colleague Sean suggested putting some open lilies in this arrangement, I preferred not to, as the lilies in bud can often give the appearance of a pod-shape. I chose a strong white pot as a solid anchor for these flowers, to give the impression that the arrangement is floating against a white wall.

STEP ONE
Cut five palm husks low (to approximately 30–40 centimetres) then place them in a white ceramic vessel (I used a 25 centimetre high x 30 centimetre diameter pot) to form a base for the arrangement. Place a stem of cordyline leaves at a right angle to the rim of the pot, trimmed so that the leaves start at the pot's edge, anchoring the husks.

STEP TWO
Place three branches of figs in between the leaves. Add one stem of nepenthes, offset to the right of the arrangement and placed so that it is facing its natural direction, to best display its beautiful tendrils.

STEP THREE
Cut the stems of two bunches of red peonies to 30–35 centimetres, then place them, stem by stem, in the centre of the arrangement. Add a few alocasia leaves as accents throughout the arrangement.

STEP FOUR
Finally, place three tight stems of lime-green lilium buds in three points (one upright, and one to each side), creating a pod-like effect.

STEP ONE
Cut one cluster (five stems) of red peonies
to approximately 30 centimetres long,
keeping the bunch bound midway with
a band of leather thonging.

STEP TWO
Leaning the blooms towards one side of
the vessel, fan them outwards to provide
an anchor for placement of all the other
peony stems, which I placed around this
initial cluster, cut in shorter lengths and
closer to the neck of the vessel.

'My inspiration: I have this very beautiful Chinese scroll painting of three peonies —
singularly my most favourite bloom — in exquisite shades of pink. When I visited Beijing
for the first time I made a pilgrimage to the Official Peony Garden (peonies are the national
flower of China) and saw some of the most magnificent specimens I have ever seen; truly
memorable, some were huge yet still looked like they had been made from the most delicate
paper. I also possess a smoke-fired, rustic vase I bought from a ceramicist in KwaZulu-
Natal, South Africa, that makes a bold, earthy contrast to the opulent beauty of peonies.'

ERIC MATTHEWS

Eric Matthews' own ceramic South African
vase. Chinese black lacquer table, Qing Dynasty
(1644–1911), and Japanese gold-leaf screen,
Meiji Period (1868–1912), from Lynette
Cunnington Chinese Art and Furniture.

144

'Even stronger than food memories are the flower memories I have of my two grandmothers. They were both fine gardeners and very proud of their prize blooms. My mother's mother, Peg, lived on a property in the southeast of South Australia. I loved watching her spread out newspaper on the kitchen table on Friday mornings in preparation for 'doing the flowers', all of which came from her garden. She taught me to make tussie mussies and posies of violets with lamb's ears.

My father's mother, Mavis, was passionate about her dahlias the size of dinner plates. But she was proudest of her cymbidium orchids — hundreds of pots — growing on stands built on the veranda of her California bungalow. These orchids (or 'awkwards', as we children called them) were breathtaking in pale pinks, deep maroons and bright greens.

While these two women definitely helped to develop my flower obsession, my friendship with Saskia has also been very influential, as we share a love of prize blooms, especially orchids and roses.'

JULIE GIBBS

STEP ONE
This vessel has a wonderful ceramic insert that is perfect for feeding blooms into to hold them in position. Initially, I created a small tussie mussie of herbs and flowers (five sprigs rosemary, three stems borage, five stems mint, six stems sage and a touch of geranium) in my hand, then placed it to the left of the ceramic insert.

STEP TWO
I then wedged a magnolia (*Magnolia grandiflora*) bloom into the right-hand edge of the insert. An air plant (tillandsia) with quite a large base made a great wedge at the back right-hand corner, behind the magnolia bloom.

STEP THREE
Next I placed two huge coral peonies (cut to approximately 20 centimetres) in the back left corner on an angle.

STEP FOUR
I added 3–5 each of 'Julia's Rose' and large pink David Austin roses, then added silver leaves of dusty miller and some pieris (lily-of-the-valley shrub) trailing under the 'Julia's Rose', as well as a single poppy. Next I inserted some sarracenia flowers in between the base flowers, along with some forget-me-nots at the front.

STEP FIVE
As a final touch, I inserted a few very beautiful anemones, one of which was stained with a dash of red. Their black, furry centres are like jewels.

Saskia Havekes' own ceramic container (a gift from Julie Gibbs). Martyn Cook Antiques.

'Gardens have always been central in my life. One of my earliest memories involves picking all the flowers in my grandmother's garden, then setting up a stall to sell them with my friend Jeanette. The first woman passing by, on her way to a nearby hospital, stopped and gave us $1 for the lot. We felt very pleased with ourselves — until my grandmother returned home to find her denuded garden.

Since then, many favourite flowers have bloomed their way into my affections. In my own garden (a former coconut plantation outside Port Vila, Vanuatu) obsessions with different plants have come and gone. One year it was waterlilies and lotuses; another, heliconias and gingers; and the next, flowering vines and climbers. This year it is flowering passionfruit. Fortunately, the 'controlled chaos look', the essence of the tropical garden, allows my past favourites to co-exist in a riot of colour and greenery.

Yet through all of these love affairs, the tuberose remains constant in my affections. My most vivid associations date from my first stay at Amandari, Adrian Zecha's wonderful tuberose-filled hotel in Ubud, Bali. Like any gardener who falls in love with a flower, I tried growing tuberose myself. I have never succeeded yet in producing stems to rival those glorious blooms in Bali. I ruefully wonder if this lack of success explains my ongoing love for the tuberose; the frustrated suitor who can't win!'

MARTIN BROWNE

Martin Browne set us an unexpectedly difficult challenge in finding the appropriate celadon-green bowl for this arrangement; they seem to be quite rare these days. The arrangement is an interpretation of the luxurious quantities of tuberose Martin so enjoyed in Bali. The Balinese tuberose has a different fragrance and is a little sparser in flowers than its Australian cousins.

STEP ONE
Fill the base of a deep round bowl with a piece of wet floral foam, cut to fit the interior of the bowl; it is fine to leave a few gaps between the foam and the bowl.

STEP TWO
Place 25 bunches (about 125 stems) of tuberose into the floral foam, inserting one stem at a time. Starting from the middle of the bowl, work your way back towards the edge until the bowl is full.

Celadon bowl from McLeod's Antiques.

STEP ONE
Half-fill a tapered cylindrical glass vase with water, then create the base arrangement by adding large tropical leaves, including alocasia, black arum and philodendron.

STEP TWO
Separate one bunch (approximately five buds) of *Magnolia grandiflora* buds into two groups, one with three buds and the other with two: it is always good to have uneven bunches of flowers. Place one to each side of the arrangement.

STEP THREE
Push two clusters of snake grass (or spear grass or fine bamboo) in amongst the leaves, to form an anchor in the centre, then add a long nepenthes (pitcher plant) stem with tendrils to shoot out from the centre of the arrangement.

STEP FOUR
Cut 5–6 lotus pods to approximately 30 centimetres, then push them in close to the leaves, so as to hide their long stems amongst the foliage.

If I was given a brief to arrange the most lush, tropical, green arrangement then this is what I would imagine. Of course, the arrangement will change over time as the magnolia blooms open. It is wonderful to see the lotus pods pushed into the leaves like large discs or buttons. The large leaf on the left has been pushed into the arrangement against its natural habit. The direction of this upright leaf helps keep the energy concentrated in the centre of the arrangement. As snake grass is a noxious weed, you might want to use either spear grass or fine bamboo instead.

It is important not to fan all the leaves out evenly around the base of the arrangement, as this would be predictable and dissipate its energy.

'Old-fashioned musk roses in shades of pink and apricot are my favourite. I like to have lots of them and put them in stubby jars and vases everywhere. They make me smile when I walk back into the house.'

ANN CHURCHILL-BROWN

Ann Churchill-Brown's taste in flowers is quite traditional and this arrangement reflects that, but the eclectic grouping of vases gives it a contemporary edge. Ann supplied three of her own vases and I matched them with a mixed selection of David Austin roses, 'Julia's Rose' and some fragrant apricot 'Just Joey' roses. The combination of colours and shapes looks very beautiful.

You could keep the vases in a cluster or separate them, putting one beside a bed, others along a mantelpiece. This Florence Broadhurst–designed wallpaper from Signature Prints makes a wonderful background because, while it is quite old-world, it is often being used today as a feature wall in contemporary spaces. The little branches coming out of the design form a crest shape around the roses, so there's that really lovely swoop, but there's also a bit of breathing space in the pattern at the top.

STEP ONE

Using a mixture of David Austin roses, 'Julia's Rose' and 'Just Joey' roses for each vase, I began by cutting down three quite large roses so they sat quite close to the rim of the vase. Most often it is better not to use three of the same kind of flower because they can end up looking like a collar.

STEP TWO

With the base roses all touching, I began feeding longer stems of roses in over the top of them. Once the roses are in each vase, you can pull them up a bit more or push them down a bit, depending on the balance.

STEP THREE

It is quite important to use some pale flowers throughout the arrangement so that it doesn't look clumsy or heavy. They're like little highlights you add to give it a bit of breathing space. I also purposely saved the pale lemon rose on the top right side till last – it is like a hero rose that makes your eye travel away from the centre of the arrangement.

Ann Churchill-Brown's own vases. 'The Cranes' wallpaper by Florence Broadhurst, courtesy of Signature Prints.

152

'It was some time in 1982 when a white potted phalaenopsis orchid landed on my *Vogue* desk, sent by the late Amana Finley, one of Sydney's great tastemakers. Not only was her gift rare and exquisite, but the magnificent spray of blooms lasted for at least six weeks, a daily reminder of the sender. Like Amana herself, this orchid was gifted with both style and substance. I never forgot that first orchid.

Since then, I have sought out orchids in ever-increasing varieties. In Sydney, working with Grandiflora, we are always searching for new orchid treasures, especially the delicate vandas.

To relax, an old friend of mine likes to clean the silver, but for me, there is nothing more therapeutic than a Saturday-morning delivery of six or so orchids and a few sheets of moss. I can while away the afternoon potting, mossing and arranging in almost every room of the house, basking in the magnificent, natural beauty of orchids.'

KARIN UPTON BAKER

Believe it or not, it took Sean and me the longest time to arrange this collection of amazing specimens. It was a challenge to get the composition right. We were so spoilt for choice with the wonderful orchids supplied; it sent us into a flat spin. Moss was flying everywhere and Sean and I kept bumping into each other.

STEP ONE
A selection of orchid plants, including vandas and phalaenopsis were placed in containers.

STEP TWO
These vessels were then placed inside a number of antique containers and then the bases were covered with moss.

Karin Upton Baker's own antique containers. Chinoiserie-style pots from Pigott's Store. 19th-century French crystal chandelier and French three-panel paper screen in background from Howell and Howell.

'When we shot in the *Vogue Living* penthouse in Sydney, each room had a very distinct look. Upon arriving, we all agreed that the "black" room would be my room to shoot in. It reminded me of the bar at Hotel Costes in Paris — dark, sexy and very moody.

The black calla lily has a dark side to it — it is a very "cabaret burlesque" flower and I always envisage it creeping about in an underground nightclub! It seems almost seedy in its ripply secrets of what's pulsating beneath. For me, with its dark sensuality, this arrangement conjures up images of a Berlin nightclub in the 1940s — I imagine Marlene Dietrich with one of these stems between her teeth.'

SEAN COOK

STEP ONE
Ten bunches of mini burgundy/black
calla lilies were trimmed to 30 centimetres,
then arranged in a cluster in a small urn
(or you could use a similar-shaped vase).

STEP TWO
Three stems of dark red anthurium
flowers were then placed at the base
of the calla lilies.

STEP THREE
Velvety black alocasia leaves were placed
at the front of the arrangement, to add an
interplay of intriguing shapes and textures
and separate the calla lilies from the edge
of the vase. These lilies make a particularly
dramatic combination with this exquisite
tabletop from The Country Trader.

William Yeonard vase. 19th-century Italian
ebonised pear wood table from The Country
Trader. *Vogue Living* penthouse, Sydney.

I find juxtaposing elements in arrangements appealing and often like to use something dried against something very lush. This arrangement typifies this aesthetic, as the velvety, dark 'Baccara' roses are contrasted with the pale and parched dried okra. The colour and tapered shape of the okra looks like an extension of the pale nude-pink calla lilies. This is a bunch of flowers I can imagine sending out on Valentine's Day — it has a very sensual quality.

STEP ONE

This arrangement was first created in the hand. I started by clustering two bunches of nude-pink calla lilies in a tight group, then added one bunch of black 'Baccara' roses (stripped of foliage and thorns and trimmed to 30 centimetre lengths).

STEP TWO

Three red peony blooms were placed at staggered heights at the front of the bouquet as a feature flower, then a few more were added to the back of the bouquet, giving a point of focus. I placed the bouquet in a round ceramic vase, half-filled with water.

STEP THREE

Two groups of 3–4 dark *Alocasia amazonia* leaves were added to the arrangement: one placed to the back left-hand side between the roses and calla lilies to sit higher than the flowers, separating the blooms and adding height; and the other to the right-hand side of the calla lilies.

STEP FOUR

I then placed two groups of approximately six dried okra pods, one to either side of the vase, arranging them so they jutted out from each side.

Ceramic pot by Gerard Havekes.

STEP ONE
I used two different vases at staggered
heights. The one in the foreground, made
by Mitchell English himself, has a very small
circular opening, great for placing a single
elegant branch of Illawarra flame tree,
allowing it to cascade out.

STEP TWO
I placed my own taller wooden bamboo-
shaped vase behind the first vase, then
filled it with another, more upright branch
of Illawarra flame tree.

'An interesting synergy occurs when marrying a synthetic/man-made material with an organic/natural object, such as in this still life. The man-made sometimes surpasses the natural for beauty. Is this image a case in point? I suppose so. After all, I'm a little biased towards wallpaper; I use it in my work. In this arrangement, the eye never rests comfortably on the subject matter; instead it moves uneasily over the entire image.

As partial as I am to the immediacy of photography and the fact that it can capture a defining moment in nature, as Gary has done here, the deception/seduction of the unreal over the real (synthetic versus organic) interests me far more.'

MITCHELL ENGLISH

1960s black velvet flocking on shellac.
Vase by Mitchell English. Saskia Havekes'
own wooden vase.

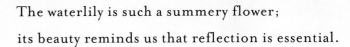

The waterlily is such a summery flower;
its beauty reminds us that reflection is essential.

This beautiful ceramic ripple vase by Bob Steiner was a gift from my former business partner, Eva Seltner. Its shape is conducive to holding groups of flowers upright. Paper or floral foam can be pushed into the vase to hold the flowers in position.

STEP ONE
Three bunches (about 15 stems) of waterlilies were held in a bundle, then fed into the vase. I cut their ends to re-open the stems and allow them to take up fresh water.

STEP TWO
I then placed two ligularia leaves on the right-hand side of the vase, to pose as a waterlily pad; waterlily pads do not survive as cut leaves.

STEP THREE
Even though I carefully placed the waterlilies in the vase, they like to bend and move of their own accord over time, creating lovely arches in their stems.

Ceramic vase by Bob Steiner.

When using ceramic vessels which could
leak or damage if directly filled with water,
we often place the flowers and water in a
vase, then insert the vase into the ceramic
vessel. I placed approximately 5 bunches
of watermelon-coloured dahlias into the
right-hand side of a tall, tapered vase set
inside the leaf vessel. I kept the dahlias in
uneven bunches as I wanted to achieve an
undulating effect by creating a few empty
pockets and rises.

STEP TWO

I then collected a huge bundle
(approximately 50 stems) of milkweed
(*Asclepias* sp. seed pods) and pushed the
trimmed stems in one large cluster into
the other side of the vase. Keeping both
the dahlias and milkweed separately
clustered in huge bunches rather than
evenly spread gives the arrangement a
bold and graphic appearance of plenty.

When I first saw this acanthus-leaf vessel, made by a lady in
Brussels, at The Country Trader in Sydney's Waterloo, I was
over the moon with excitement. I was intrigued to discover
that these large leaves were a relief which were then adhered
onto a plain ceramic pot. We were kindly lent two of these
to put in our shop window display for a month; they caused
a huge stir with our customers and were much loved.

People have mixed feelings about dahlias — they are
either loved or strongly disliked. These watermelon dahlias
have a terrific shape and summery colour. Best kept in
large groups for maximum impact, when coupled with
the lime-green of milkweed they remind me of the skin
of a watermelon. Thinking about how things occur
in nature — like here, with the replication of the contrasting
colours of watermelon and its skin — is always a great source
of inspiration when working with flowers.

Belgian acanthus leaf vessel and c. 1870
French marble butcher's table from The
Country Trader.

164

'If I think back to the flowers of my childhood, the opening image is of a tiny rose. I wore a small cluster of these in my hair when playing a fairy or an angel, aged about six; my first appearance on a stage. The roses made an impact. Their perfume, so hard to describe and impossible to forget, is still with me. It evokes a soft emotional response, a poignancy for that little girl, so innocent and excited by her first concert appearance. The roses in a cluster were tiny: perfect palest pink, feminine. They are hard to find now; I never see them.

I have long wanted a climbing vine of 'Cécile Brünner' roses, but have never made the effort. The perfume is mercifully not sweet but musky, tremulous, haunting, only just present. They speak of another time: when girls in cream muslin dresses and long hair walked beneath arbours in large gardens, carrying small, neat books in which a tiny rose was pressed. It is helpful to have an image of a healthy rose vine: a tangled mass of buds over an arch in a garden or around a post on a veranda, or glimpsed through a window. In years ahead, when time is a gift available each day, I might find the specialist nursery where these precious flowers are nurtured and bring one home to embark on a rose-growing project.'

ROBYN NEVIN

This ficus screen seemed so appropriate for interpreting the wayward nature of the 'Cécile Brünner' rose. Its wooden vine structure provided a wonderful base for creating a climbing arrangement, echoing the way the roses grow.

STEP ONE
I cut approximately 15–20 bunches of these roses to 15–20 centimetres and cleared their bases of leaves and thorns.

STEP TWO
Then I created clusters by placing the stem ends (approximately 5 per cluster, or half a bunch of roses) in water vials.

STEP THREE
These clusters were then wedged in a trailing pattern into the twisted ficus screen base and secured with wire.

STEP FOUR
Finally, I interspersed individual David Austin roses amongst the 'Cécile Brünner' roses, to add a diversity of shapes and sizes. The water vials attached to the groups of stems on the reverse side of the ficus screen kept the flowers fresh for days.

The Alvar Aalto vase was the inspiration for this arrangement — it is superb when filled with masses of the same type of flower, such as tulips or, in this instance, bromeliads. Its appeal is that you can hardly tell there's a vase there. The flowers look free-standing, while the vase seems to hug the flowers into a very particular shape; it's wonderful to see the beauty of the stems. Usually we wouldn't put extra leaves in this vase, but on this occasion, it seemed like the arrangement needed a contrasting shape.

STEP ONE

Cut handfuls of bromeliad stems to a similar length, then push them into the curves of a wide vase such as this Alvar Aalto vase, which has been three-quarters filled with water.

STEP TWO

Place large green leaves such as ornamental grape leaves to the right of the arrangement, trailing over the side of the vase.

iittala Alvar Aalto vase.

Take one bunch (approximately 5 stems) of *Magnolia grandiflora* foliage and cut the stems to various lengths between 20 and 35 centimetres. Sit them in a tall, round vase half-filled with water, then feed in 10 stems of smoke bush (*Cotinus coggygria*) foliage, keeping them long and lyrical to stand quite high above the flowers.

STEP TWO

Place approximately three hydrangea flowers throughout the base provided by the greenery, then add 20–30 individual roses that have been stripped of their thorns and leaves to halfway up their stems. I used lemon 'Elina' roses and orange 'Redgold' roses but you could use a mixture of your favourite roses.

STEP THREE

Place one *Magnolia grandiflora* flower at the base of the arrangement on the right-hand side, then add five striped anthurium flowers across the centre.

STEP FOUR

Place 3–5 stems of viburnum berries trailing in groups from the base of the arrangement.

This is what I would call a more traditional arrangement. The striped anthurium flowers are relatively new to our market. They add an intriguing element, along with the yellow and red viburnum berries, which we always have in the shop around December. The vessel, a Venini vase by Fulvio Bianconi, was scaled, curled black glass from Murano purchased by one of our clients from a limited-edition series. The combination of differently coloured roses pushes this arrangement a little bit further. Had we used all the same coloured rose, it would have made the arrangement look too bland and obvious. The smoke bush foliage creates terrific height and is a well-loved and reliable tool we often use at Grandiflora.

Leo Schofield's own Venini vase, by Fulvio Bianconi, and Japanese screen. Home of Leo Schofield.

'As a young girl, I'd go for bushwalks with my grandfather on his property in Western Australia. We loved collecting exquisite native flowers and then making pressings of them. My grandfather would ensure each flower was perfectly preserved in his self-made press. He knew every plant's name, in Latin as well, and I'd write the flower's name on each page, in my neatest print. When they were dried, he would meticulously bind them together into a small, perfect book. I am fortunate that my dear grandfather passed his affection for the bush on to me in such a special way.'

MELISSA HASLUCK

STEP ONE
Start by placing two stems of gum blossom (*Eucalyptus youngiana*) at opposite ends of a wide 35 centimetre tall vase; one on a 45 degree angle, the other horizontal to the table.

STEP TWO
Place two generous bunches of leucadendron divided into two groups of five stems each around the vase, then cut four large red ginger flowers (*Alpinia purpurata*) to approximately 55 centimetres and insert three of them in the centre of the arrangement. I placed the other red ginger flower separately as it is important to place odd numbers of flowers in their areas.

STEP THREE
Nestle two bunches of waterlilies into the front and side of the arrangement. Separate three bunches of grevillea, then add the stems to the sides, one at a time.

STEP FOUR
As a final touch, I added a stem of magnolia in bud with excellent foliage to the right and leaning towards the top of the arrangement.

The lotus flower warrants meditation — it conjures up a mood of serenity and simplicity. It is a very 'Zen' flower; beautiful in all its forms, but especially when it is in bud. At Grandiflora we often peel the petals back ourselves or sometimes tuck them in towards the centre of the flower. When Gary and I first travelled to Bali, in the honeymoon period of our budding relationship, he managed to con me into slipping into the water of a lotus pond as big as a football oval, in my underwear. When my feet made it to the bottom, I was up to my knees in mud and could only feel lotus roots between my toes. He asked me to lie back in the water and look as relaxed as I could. I could only think of the eels living in that squelching mud — quite revolting. It must have been love! And a passion for the lotus flower itself.

STEP ONE
Take two bunches of ligularia leaves (approximately 12 stems), then place them interlocking around the neck of a ceramic oil jar or similarly shaped vase, forming a tight cabbage shape.

STEP TWO
Cut three lotus flowers to the same height as the vase, then push them into the tight formation of ligularia leaves to form a strong base for the arrangement. Turn back some of the outer lotus petals to open up the blooms.

STEP THREE
Feed in a few more lotus blooms (I used another 3 stems) adding them at irregular heights. Add a few (say 2) lotus flower buds to give the arrangement the appearance of a living, growing entity.

STEP FOUR
Add some lotus pods as a final touch. Here I used nine, placing them in positions which best showcased the natural movement of their stems.

French wheel-thrown glazed terracotta ball pot, French oak table and 19th-century French lock-printed paper screen from The Country Trader.

'My most inspiring flower? No question about it. *Magnolia grandiflora*. I've had one in every garden I've owned. Once I moved an ailing eighty-year-old specimen from Cammeray to Woollahra and it not only survived but flourished triumphantly. I love everything about this tree; its form, the leaves like shiny dark green patent leather, the undersides a beautiful khaki suede. Then there are the flowers, great creamy chalices, the petals as soft as kid gloves. Now there are many trees with lovely flowers and a few might challenge the magnolia for beauty, but the magnolia has a third ace up its sleeve – fragrance. Not any old fragrance, but a heady lemony one. On a tree the flowers look splendid, but who has ever owned one and been able to resist breaking off a branch or two and bringing it inside to put in a big vase, allowing the scent to fill the room? There are other gorgeous magnolias, most notably the spectacular pink *M. campbellii*, but in this family, *grandiflora* is king.'

LEO SCHOFIELD

These beautiful flowers are our signature bloom and I was so impressed when Leo Schofield chose it as one of his favourites. I enjoy our chats filled with great flower enthusiasm every morning when he walks past the shop, especially hearing about his emerging garden in Tasmania. His Venini vase is of pale wisteria-coloured glass, copied from one in a painting by Veronese.

STEP ONE
Trim one stem of *Magnolia grandiflora* with its foliage intact to 55 centimetres.

STEP TWO
Quarter-fill a vase with water, then place the *Magnolia grandiflora* in the vase, resting it on the front rim. With such a simple arrangement, the water must be filled to an elegant level and not look too overflowing or bulky. Too much water is wasteful and harder to change, which is vital for the longevity of the flower.

Leo Schofield's own Venini vase.
Home of Leo Schofield.

Utilising large, compact groups of violet leaves can be a saviour for many arrangements. They enhance all flowers, adding a sense of lushness and luxuriousness.

STEP ONE
Starting with this beautiful glass urn, I placed three bunches of violet leaves around the rim of the urn, leaving a few gaps to break the line.

STEP TWO
I then added a trail of giant honeysuckle (*Lonicera hildebrandiana*), arranging it so that some swirled into and around the urn, trailing over its edge.

STEP THREE
As a final touch, I added five trimmed evergreen magnolia (*Magnolia grandiflora* 'Little Gem') buds in groups to the left and right of the arrangement, finishing with two bunches (approximately 10 stems) of gardenias, which I placed in the centre of the urn.

'I am obsessed with the purity and timelessness of a white flower. Magnolias and gardenias are my favourites. I love filling our home with them, and always have bunches in small round glass vases dotted throughout our home. I buy extra magnolia foliage to fill my bouquets. I also love the smell of star jasmine. It reminds me of my childhood; long, hot, happy Queensland summers.'

HEIDI MIDDLETON

Glass urn, 19th-century four-panel paper screen and 1930s Art Deco bureau from The Country Trader.

The inspiration for this arrangement came solely from an ethereal floral wall mural, created by Ebony Bizys of *Vogue Living* magazine. Inspired by the works of artist Hiroshi Sugito and Cy Twombly, the mural incorporates sorbet-coloured hues with wispy, whimsical marks such as stylised flower stencils and elements of collaged floral wallpapers. There are small personal references hidden behind the fluffy, cloud-like shapes throughout the work. There couldn't have been a more perfect flower than these large pink peonies placed in three William Yeonard vases. It was important to place the flowers just under the little bird perched on its branch to form the perfect composition.

STEP ONE

I started by collecting three glass vases, all of different heights, then half-filled them with water. I then gathered 10–15 stems of large pink peonies.

STEP TWO

Next, I chose a fully blown 'hero' bloom for the shorter vase and cut it short, leaving the foliage intact, so the base of the flower sat in the neck of the container – this is an important feature flower as it makes the eye travel down across all the blooms, and anchors the entire arrangement.

STEP THREE

I then trimmed the remaining peony stems to 20–25 centimetres and placed them in groups of three in each of the two remaining vases. I placed some flowers facing forwards and others at different angles. Sometimes it is lovely to also see the side and back of some flowers; it is not always vital to see the front of every flower displayed.

STEP FOUR

Due to the beautiful backdrop, I decided to keep all the vases clustered together in a group. However, this arrangement could also be separated, with the vases placed individually around a room or down the centre of a table for a dinner party – in this case, cut down the taller blooms so they do not obstruct your guests' vision.

Glass vases by William Yeonard. Floral wall mural in background by Ebony Bizys. *Vogue Living* penthouse, Sydney.

'My favourite flower is the waterlily. Recently I bought four big buds and studied them as they opened. I like their simple symmetrical faces, the delicate pink stain of the petals and the brightness of their green stems.

Three bloomed and one didn't. I don't know why it didn't. I filled the water in the vase high so they bobbed on top. I was happy every day the other three were blooming. I carried the vase into my office and back into the living room. I didn't want to miss any time with them. To me, they are proof of the divine in life, of simple miracles.'

JANE CAMPION

Waterlilies tend to close in the late afternoon, so unfortunately they do not make such a good flower for an evening party. They are best kept in a group so that all the flowers push into each other when they open up. The backs are also beautiful, with their deep brown skins. As an aquatic plant, waterlilies like plenty of water, so be sure to place the flowers close to the top of the vase and keep the water level high.

STEP ONE
Take 3–4 bunches of waterlilies and trim their stems to 30 centimetres. Cluster them together in your hand first, then, use the other hand to arrange the flowers, forming them into a good shape by pulling some a little higher and pushing others a little lower. Using cord, string or a rubber band, tie the stems together just underneath the flower heads. Be careful not to tie them too tightly.

STEP TWO
Place the group of flowers into a vase filled almost to the top with water. Rearrange the flowers slightly until the shape is visually pleasing. Alternatively, use a vessel with quite a narrow neck that will be able to support the stems comfortably.

Anatolian antique door and Tokat water jar from Orientalia.

STEP ONE
Cut the elastic bands off two bunches
of variegated hosta leaves, then lay the
bunches on an angle to one side of a
trough vase filled two-thirds full of water.

STEP TWO
Cut one bunch of sarracenia (pitcher plant)
stems to 20 centimetres, then poke groups
of them at different heights into the other
side of the vase, so they appear to float
above the leaves.

'I consider myself very fortunate to be able to go to work
and be surrounded by the beautiful and unusual sights
and smells of the amazing flowers that come into the
Grandiflora shop. Every day offers a different experience.'

JOHANNA DETMOLD

STEP ONE
Take four bunches of *Hydrangea paniculata*, bundle them tightly in one group, then place them in a low, round vase on a table.

STEP TWO
Place two bunches of large antique hydrangeas at a right angle, up against the *Hydrangea paniculata* and leaning out of the right-hand side of the vase.

STEP THREE
Place some individual snail begonia leaf stems between the two groups of hydrangeas, to provide shape, colour and texture to the arrangement. The snail begonia leaf is so decorative it can pose as an alternative to a flower.

STEP FOUR
Finally, place approximately twelve white anthurium flowers across the top of the arrangement.

Hydrangea paniculata is my favourite hydrangea. It has a magnificent panicle. Coupling it with these autumn-toned antique hydrangeas (which are also beautiful dried), it gives this arrangement a bulky, luxurious size. We always have clients who are interested in the antique hydrangea and get very excited when its season arrives. The snail begonia leaf has to be the feature of this arrangement; I cut it directly from a pot plant and placed it like a big brooch at the front of the vase. But it is the white anthuriums that transform this composition from being bulky to elegant. They needed to stand slightly above the other flowers to give them some breathing space; they appear to dance like butterflies or birds above the other blooms.

Home of Elizabeth Jones.

STEP ONE
Gather a single, perfect deep red rose
stem in full bloom, then trim the stem
to 25 centimetres and remove
the thorns and most of the foliage.

STEP TWO
Place the rose in a tall vase with
a narrow neck.

'There is a glass cabinet in my living room in which I like to place things that you wouldn't normally find in a cabinet: things that I find; pieces from my travels, such as a collection of iridescent carnival glasses. In one of these, I'll place a red rose. When the cabinet is illuminated, the glasses become almost 'day-glo' and the red rose 'sings'. It is like a living still-life.

I adore armfuls of gnarled garden roses in large crystal vases. They remind me of my mother and grandmother growing them during my childhood in the west of New South Wales; their big, magnificent heads growing out of the dusty, burned earth. Their colours are beautiful and their smell is to-die-for, but what I love most about them are their imperfections.'

SHARYN STORRIER LYNEHAM

'Some of my most treasured memories are intricately related to flowers.

Wild orchids remind me of my granny, mum's mother, and time spent with her in Paraguay, while hydrangeas take me back to the many summer holidays spent with my father's parents at their beach house in Argentina. As a child, the hydrangea surrounding the house towered above us and, with its beautiful hues of pinks and blues, provided great hiding spots! There were always flowers in this house; a happy, casual mix of garden roses in every colour and, of course, hydrangeas.

My mother has a green thumb and a natural talent for arranging flowers. She is a generous woman, with a strong sense of community, and I've watched her make hundreds of arrangements. So when I got married there was only *one* person I wanted to make my bouquet. An informal, soft mix of local jasmine, wisteria, delicate white orchids and wild flowers; it was perfect. And then my mum went ahead and decorated the whole church as well!

Then once, at the end of a grey day in Milan, I returned home to find the hallway bursting with the most glorious, fragrant roses — I could hardly get in the door! Every vase was full, every surface covered — I couldn't believe it. They were so stunning, with their different stem-lengths, varieties and colours; such abundance was quite overwhelming. In the kitchen all the pots and pans were full of roses as well — and the bathtub and the bedroom! Paolo had been to every florist in Milan; I was the only one receiving roses that day.

Now, I am enchanted by Australian flora; such fascinating forms. Not just the stunning flowers but also the pods, the seeds and the shapes of the leaves — all so interesting and unique. They are the start of many more wonderful memories.'

ALEXIA GNECCHI RUSCONE

STEP ONE
Place two stems of hakea seed pods to the front right-hand side of a tall, narrow vase, leaning on a slight angle.

STEP TWO
Add a whole bunch of pink and red gum flowers (*Eucalyptus ficifolia*), clustered in a tight group to the left-hand side of the vase.

STEP THREE
Add three stems of large gum nuts to the back of the vase, leaning against the back rim. Finally, add large mallee gum blossom buds (such as *Eucalyptus youngiana*) to the front of the vase.

Alexia Gnecchi Ruscone's own coffee table.
Oil painting by P. Drummond.
Vase handmade by Alexia Gnecchi Ruscone, with surface shaped using a beach pebble.

Cut three stems of white Christmas bush
to 60 centimetres, then place them to the
left-hand side of a cube vase. Cross these
stems with a few dogwood branches to
the right-hand side. These two elements
form an excellent base.

STEP TWO
Place ten stems (about 2 bunches)
of white peonies amongst the Christmas
bush and dogwood stems.

STEP THREE
Tuck in the occasional stem of 'Sahara' rose
(I used approximately 10 stems throughout).

'The perfume of summer's flowers, very much the
perfume after a long, white winter, brings signs
of a lightness of life and memories of childhood.'
ALICE ALEXANDER

Home of Alice and John Alexander.

'My first *Gardenia* 'Magnifica' was given to me in a cellophane box by an adolescent schoolboy, awkward in a borrowed dinner suit and his father's bow tie. If you were taking a girl to your school dance in early 60s Melbourne, you arrived with a corsage. They were usually frankly hideous — large slipper orchids in serviceable brown or green, wired together with a bit of fern: maidenhair if you were lucky, asparagus if you weren't. I thought them vaguely obscene, vile of colour, and, as they were devoid of perfume, not only charmless but soulless. But this lanky boy handed me two astonishingly beautiful, perfect velvety white flowers, with a fragrance so ravishing that I'm sure I blushed. It spoke of a life beyond school dances, of places warmer than the puritanical chill of Melbourne; a grown-up world of delight and danger and hot summer nights.

Despite their exquisite whiteness, there's nothing innocent about them. Look at Billie Holiday, with those eyes that had seen everything; two huge gardenias covering one side of her magnificent head, perfuming the night air as she sang of heartache and lynchings, and dead of narcotics, booze and trouble at 44.

They, like us, are mutable of course. But they fade to gold and keep their perfume to the end, reminding us of summer nights past, when the world lay all before us.'

SUZY BALDWIN

Suzy Baldwin holds the greatest passion for gardenias of anyone I know. She is berserk about them! The two of us can often be found, early on a Friday morning, pushing our noses into a bunch of them. Nothing, we agree, surpasses this, especially when the season for *Gardenia* 'Magnifica' arrives in late November.

STEP ONE
I nestled approximately seven bunches of *Gardenia* 'Magnifica' (stems trimmed to 15 centimetres and kept in bunches with rubber bands) together in a large ceramic bowl filled with water.

STEP TWO
Starting from the edge, I placed three whole bunches of these gardenias to form a base around the rim of the bowl, then continued adding a few extra bunches towards the centre until the bowl was full.

STEP THREE
A final bunch of gardenias could be separated and then each individual blooms inserted randomly amongst the bunches to create an undulating aesthetic.

Suzy Baldwin's own celadon bowl.
Mud cloth from Mali.

As this metal trough was not waterproof, I first placed a plastic container inside it, raised up higher with a layer of rolled-up newspaper (you could also use floral foam or plastic bags rolled into balls to prop up the container). This is a good technique for faking the length of flower stems in a deep container. Half-fill the container with water.

I then gathered approximately three bunches of open, soft 'Julia's Rose', then removed their thorns and most of their foliage and trimmed the stems to 40 centimetres.

I clustered them together in one large bunch, then placed them in the left-hand side of the plastic container. Next, I gently pushed the front three or so roses down so the flower heads were just above the rim of the trough, then pulled some of the back roses a little higher, spreading them apart slightly.

Finally, I added a whole bunch of decorative berries to the right-hand side of the container; they were secured in place by the narrowness of the trough's opening.

'I love the contrast of the delicate papery petals of the 'Julia's Rose' against this rusted metal trough container from Alison Coates. Due to its soft, unusual, pale coffee colour, this rose is a favourite bridesmaids' flower. Before I worked at Grandiflora I never really appreciated roses — it is only since then that I've come across garden roses in all their glory and seen them for their unadulterated beauty.'

SEAN COOK

'As a young adult, I travelled around southern England with my grandfather. We visited many stately gardens of old English manors and castles. In one such highly manicured garden, overwhelmed by yet another abundance of beautiful roses, I remember protesting to my grandfather, "I prefer more exotic flowers, like lilies." He replied with a wink, "Ah, the roses and raptures of virtue, the lilies and languor of vice."

Years later, having seen so many varieties of stunning roses come through Grandiflora, I've gained a new appreciation for this classic beauty. I've also come to relish how exotic and unusual flowers can combine strikingly with the more classic blooms, in a rebellious expression of wildness of spirit, just as virtue and vice can exist side by side.'

MELISSA HASLUCK

STEP ONE
To start building the base of this arrangement, gather two clusters of hydrangeas, then place a sweep of artichokes (cut to about 40 centimetres) running through the vase. Place them in a group quite close to the neck of a wide-necked medium (30 centimetres-tall) vase.

STEP TWO
Push in three groups of cockscomb celosia, in bunches of five stems, placing one at the back of the vase, then add approximately five alocasia leaves.

STEP THREE
Start introducing the other flowers once the base is complete. I added three large heads of hydrangeas, along with about two bunches of tiger orchids, which I placed in a group to each side. I then anchored in three lotus pods (beautiful with their open seed cases).

STEP FOUR
The final accent was the sweeping branch of bean-like pods (from senna). I then added a few large, firm and flat leather leaves to the front and sides of the arrangement.

STEP ONE

These roses came in bundles picked
from the growers' driveway. I left
a lot of their foliage and thorns on,
only stripping halfway up the stems.

STEP TWO

I then placed the roses in the vessel
(in this case a copper-glazed bowl)
in groups of 20 stems at a time,
building up the volume as I added
more flowers.

STEP THREE

Once all the stems were placed in
the vase, I pulled some blooms out
so that they protruded and left others
recessed to create a sense of undulation,
as it is lovely to see flowers as they would
grow in nature.

The 'Tineke' rose has a green overtone. Lorna and Barry Osborne grow these roses near
the Olympic stadium in Sydney. They pride themselves on growing their roses for us so
they appear wayward and unpredictable, like true garden roses; not like the uniformity
of conventional glasshouse roses. The luxurious antique walnut armoire in the background
provided a dramatic contrast for the brilliance of the flowers. The arrangement almost
seems to be part of the doors because there is so much floral detail carved into them.
My aim here was to encourage people not only to think of an arrangement itself,
but also to consider the environment into which it is to be placed and how this
impacts on the overall look of the flowers.

Copper-glazed fuji bowl.
18th-century Spanish oak chopping table.
Louis XIV period walnut armoire from
The Country Trader.

Cut five frangipani branches to
45 centimetres (about two-thirds higher
than the containers you plan to use).
Lean each stem against the edge of the
neck of the vessel, creating balance.

STEP TWO
Slide a few shorter branches into the centre
of the vessels to fill any gaps. Keep this
arrangement loose and not contrived,
as this is important to reflect the nature
of these flowers.

'Frangipanis are my favourite flowers because they herald
summer with their lovely smell as their petals make patterns
in my garden before I collect them and put them in water
for a day or two. They also remind me of my mother and
father because they formed Mum's wedding bouquet. She
wore one in her hair and Dad one in his buttonhole in the
photograph of their marriage, when they were so young and
hopeful. My choice of container would be an orange enamel
jug, in Rajasthan colours.'

JAN CHAPMAN

Enamel coffee pot and soup
terrine from Mark Conway.

'This strong, sculptural arrangement looks as if it could be growing on the side of a tree — like an abstract epiphyte. I love how the callas appear to be growing out of this piece of bark. The shape and texture of the bark were the initial inspiration for this arrangement, but the bright yellow contrast of the calla lilies brings it to life. Keeping the calla lilies massed in groups adds an element of roundness to counterbalance the strength of the bark shapes, while the texture of the succulent has a scaly, ruffled appearance which sits well against the simplicity of the calla lilies. I am always drawn to strong sculptural forms.'

SEAN COOK

STEP ONE
I started by fastening two large slabs of bark (I would use hard iron or paperbark for an arrangement like this) on an angle around a rectangular glass vase, using leather thonging.

STEP TWO
I then half-filled the vase with water and placed three different-sized pieces of bark in the vase so they protruded at varying angles.

STEP THREE
Next I placed approximately five bunches of yellow calla lilies (trimmed to 60 centimetres) in two groups; one on each side of the central bark slab.

STEP FOUR
To create an intriguing texture, I added a few pieces of black rosette succulent (*Aeonium* 'Zwartkop') to the left-hand side of the vase.

STEP FIVE
Finally, I interspersed two groups, each containing 6–10 ctenanthe leaves amongst the bark and calla lilies, to simulate the appearance of a growing plant.

STEP ONE

Start with 4–5 stems of *Magnolia* 'Little Gem' foliage, keeping them quite long (approximately 45 centimetres). Place magnolia foliage at angles into the vase.

STEP TWO

Feed in the burgundy ctenanthe leaves throughout the magnolia foliage, placing them so they sweep down towards the table.

STEP THREE

Place one bunch (5 stems) of autumn-coloured hydrangea heads (cut down to 30 centimetres) lower than the magnolia stems and interspersed throughout the greenery, thereby forming a strong base.

STEP FOUR

Feed in approximately five pink waterlilies to the right of the vase, in amongst the hydrangeas. Add three stems of phalaenopsis orchids, to stand upright in the centre, and a couple of banksia nuts nestled in as a surprise element.

Inspiration for this arrangement came from this unusual Copeland and De Soos vase (a gift from my dear friend Julie Gibbs) coupled with the muted colouring and shapes in the backdrop. There is a hazy quality in both the vase and the background fabric. The flowers really leap off the page.

We call these banksia nuts 'upholstery nuts' because they look and feel as if they are covered in upholstery fabric.

'Leda' by Decortex fabric in background from Brunschwig and Fils. Copeland and De Soos vase.

'Peonies would have to be amongst my favourite flowers as they represent the birth of our second daughter, Ines. When each of our daughters was born we filled the house with different flowers to welcome them into the world (and they were all from Grandiflora!). Flowers represent these very special times in our lives and on each of the girls' birthdays we fill the house with their flowers again to remind us of this.'

BILL GRANGER

STEP ONE

There is nothing quite as luxurious as this mass of white peonies. What makes them even more special is that they usually only flower for a few weeks each year, starting in mid-November. Keeping approximately five stems together in bunches, I started to build up a large group in one hand, placing the flowers at varying heights.

STEP TWO

When I had formed a bouquet of approximately 25 stems, I trimmed the stems until they were almost even at about 35 centimetres long.

STEP THREE

I then placed the bouquet in a glass vase, filled two-thirds with water (you can first tie the stems together with green ribbon), then added approximately 5–10 extra stems around and throughout this initial group, to create an undulation and puffiness to the blooms, without them appearing like a tight ball.

'I believe the scent of a flower is its soul. Jasmine and gardenias have an innocence and freshness that is both appealing and invigorating. As soon as I inhale their sweet aroma, I know that summer is on its way. A sense of excitement soon follows, as there is no better way to spend the summer season than in this glorious city of Sydney.'

GUILLAUME BRAHIMI

STEP ONE
Holding one large bunch of jasmine at its base, push the stems deep into a tall vase, letting the top trail over the edge of the container.

STEP TWO
Using 2–3 large bunches of trimmed gardenias, insert each bunch to one side of the jasmine base.

STEP THREE
Finally, clean the foliage from 2–3 edible, unripe fig branches and slot them into the arrangement, just off the centre.

Window screen and Turkish yoghurt pot from Orientalia.

Fill a cube vase three-quarters with water. Start forming the base structure of the arrangement using two bunches of hydrangeas whose stems have been trimmed to 25 centimetres. Keep each bunch in clusters of five stems per bunch, then place one bunch on each side of the vase.

STEP TWO

Wedge two bunches of buddleia on either side of the hydrangeas, then push in five monstera fruits (whose stems have been trimmed to 20–30 centimetre lengths and foliage removed) to anchor the arrangement.

STEP THREE

Place three stems of smoke bush (*Cotinus coggygria*) foliage around the base of the arrangement, creating the illusion that it is growing in clusters out from the hydrangeas. Add three philodendron leaves to the right of the arrangement.

STEP FOUR

Push the trimmed stems of one bunch of red peonies into the arrangement in an undulating form: some below the monstera fruits, some protruding and others recessed, so they appear as if they are growing out from the leaves and fruit.

STEP FIVE

Place one pale peony in the centre of the arrangement. This acts as a focal flower, breaking up the boldness of the more richly coloured red peonies.

Even though these aren't tropical flowers, this arrangement has a warm-climate feeling to it. I envisage that it could have been picked out of a garden in Queensland; the peonies, of course, would have had to be flown in from colder climes. The lushness of these peonies helps to transform the arrangement from being flat in tone, while the monstera (*Monstera deliciosa*) fruits are an interesting surprise, cut down low for the eye to find. Buddleia is a butterfly attractant.

This tropical arrangement is a good example of clustering a number of elements together. These heliconias are transformed by cutting them down, then layering them in large groups. I often like to form pockets of leaves around groups of flowers. Although I am generally not a great fan of variegated leaves, the yellow stripes in this ginger foliage encourage the eye to move around the arrangement. Rolls of banana leaves are economical and easily obtained from an Asian vegetable market. The bulrushes, cut down low and pushed underneath the heliconias, add an intriguing element. As snake grass is now classified as a noxious weed, you might want to use spear grass or fine bamboo instead.

It isn't essential to see each element immediately. Often elements can be clustered at the back of an arrangement or placed down low; they don't always need to be fanned out higher than the flowers at the front. To me, it is always important to leave breathing space between the wall and the flowers.

STEP ONE
Cut ten stems of variegated ginger leaves to 70 centimetres. Place them in a chunky cylindrical container; here, I have used a rustic French confit jar.

STEP TWO
Form three groups of bulrushes (five heads per group) in your hand, then push each group down in between the ginger leaves.

STEP THREE
Next, form two groups of yellow heliconias (one group of ten, the other of five) then place the larger group to one side of the arrangement, resting against the neck of the vase. Place the other group in the centre of the arrangement, slightly higher than the first. A third smaller group is tucked in low to the left to provide balance.

STEP FOUR
Create three groups of snake grass (or use spear grass or fine bamboo instead) cut to 90 centimetres, then place them on a slant between the groups of heliconias.

STEP FIVE
Take three bundles of rolled banana leaves, then place one sitting down low in the centre of the arrangement, with the remaining two bundles sitting on the table to the left-hand side of the container.

STEP SIX
Finally, to add an element of shadowing, place a few dark philodendron leaves at the left-hand base of the arrangement.

19th-century French confit jar and 19th-century blue file box from The Country Trader.

Fill a small plastic container (a takeaway container will do) three-quarters full of water and secure it inside a coral base or a similar-sized vessel. Trim all the frangipani branches to 25 centimetres or so and allow the ends to emit a little sap before placing them into the water. These branches will form the base of your arrangement.

STEP TWO
Nestle in three lotus pods at slightly different heights; this evokes a more natural effect amongst the frangipani leaves and flowers, creating added depth and interest. Remember to add the flowers and pods not just in the front but also at the sides and back.

STEP THREE
Finally, add two lotus flowers, keeping one that is slightly more open to be the main feature of the piece.

'Love for the beauty of flowers will be with me forever. An intoxicating, beautiful bloom excites the senses and gives me the inspiration and pleasure that only nature can provide.

From making flower mud pies or picking blossoms from the garden then spraying them with hairspray, through to cutting armloads of azaleas from our wonderful rambling garden, my passion for flowers has always been encouraged since childhood.'

MICHELLE CAMBRIDGE

Michelle Cambridge's own coral vessel.

The calla lily seems to have become the signature flower of Jeff Leatham, Artistic Director and florist for the Four Seasons George V Hotel in Paris. He is famous for submerging them upside-down in water-filled glass vases. Nowadays, we find them in a range of colour combinations, often with the leaf growing through the flower as some sort of weird adaptation. Large quantities of calla lilies like this are very expensive, but they have excellent longevity. The mango-coloured ones always herald summer in Australia. They make a wonderful specimen flower and look superb in groups leaning on an angle out of a simple glass vase.

STEP ONE
Start with ten bunches of burgundy calla lilies, with their green leaf tips intact, and three bunches of pale pink calla lilies, stems of each trimmed to 40 centimetres. Some of the pink lilies are to be threaded through the centre of the arrangement.

STEP TWO
Keep the bunches of burgundy calla lilies together, tightly clustered and chunky, then tie them together with a soft cord or ribbon, taking care as the stems are quite fragile and crush easily. Place this large bunch of burgundy calla lilies at the front of a large vase with a narrow neck, tilting it slightly towards the right.

STEP THREE
As a finishing touch, gently lay the remaining pink calla lilies, tied together as an entire bunch, horizontally across the top of the arrangement, with the blooms facing left and the stems facing right.

Écoute-Moi vase by Christian Tortu and painting by Makinti Napanangka (© the artist licensed by Aboriginal Artists Agency 2006) from Macleay on Manning.

STEP ONE
Take two groups of gigantic upright tropical leaves, then criss-cross them and place them into a trough vase. Roll one of the groups of leaves to create a secure area to place the smaller variegated alocasia leaves against.

STEP TWO
Take six dark red torch ginger flowers, with their stems cut to various lengths, then place them in a line across the middle of the vase.

STEP THREE
Insert three anthurium flowers into the arrangement – two to the front left-hand side and one at the back, above the space behind the ginger flowers.

In working with flowers, I've found that, like so many things in life, people often want what they can't have. Those of us who live in more temperate climes especially treasure the lushness of tropical leaves and beauty of tropical flowers, like the bold leaves and striking flowers used here. Those in tropical areas, however, covet peonies and other cooler-climate blooms. Living in a water-poor environment, I foresee a time when such blooms will become difficult to procure — and even in my own garden, I've moved towards growing hardy succulents and plants with drought-tolerant foliage.

we would like to thank

A very special thank you to Sean Cook, without whose support and enthusiasm
this book would have been impossible to produce.

I also wish to thank our publisher, Julie Gibbs, for her vision and friendship,
as well as the tireless and dedicated Penguin crew: Adam Laszczuk, Deborah Brash,
Nicole Brown, Ingrid Ohlsson, Alison Cowan, Nicola Young and, especially, our
editor, Kathleen Gandy. Thanks, as well, to Jennifer Stackhouse and Del Thomas
for bringing their botanical expertise to the project.

Special thanks must go to the Grandiflora team: Julia Parker, May Lloyd,
Genevieve Freeman, Johanna Detmold, Lucinda Johnson, Melissa Hasluck,
Janet Pankoff and Effi Voss.

Thanks also to our families, with special thanks to Louise Walker,
Anna-Maryke Grey, Ineke Souris and our daughters Sunday, Ginger and Ruby.

I wish to thank our growers, especially Craig Scott, Darren Butler,
Lawrence and Anna Leoncino, Nick and Paula Burchell, Gowan Stewart,
Phillip Miscuso and Serina Alesci.

Thanks must also go to the people who generously supplied locations for
many of the shoots: Danika Jones and David Clarke, residents at Macleay Regis,
Jill and Rod Ordish, Elizabeth Jones and Geoff Clarke.

Special thanks to those who provided support for Gary: Toby Dixon,
James Fisher and Pix Photo Media.

And finally, heartfelt thanks to Eva Seltner and Alison Coates, who helped me
lay my foundations as a florist, and to the inspiring Yolande Gray and Prue Rushton.

index

LANTERN

Published by the Penguin Group
Penguin Group (Australia)
250 Camberwell Road, Camberwell, Victoria 3124, Australia
(a division of Pearson Australia Group Pty Ltd)
Penguin Group (USA) Inc.
375 Hudson Street, New York, New York 10014, USA
Penguin Group (Canada)
90 Eglinton Avenue East, Suite 700, Toronto, Canada ON M4P 2Y3
(a division of Pearson Penguin Canada Inc.)
Penguin Books Ltd
80 Strand, London WC2R 0RL England
Penguin Ireland
25 St Stephen's Green, Dublin 2, Ireland
(a division of Penguin Books Ltd)
Penguin Books India Pvt Ltd
11 Community Centre, Panchsheel Park, New Delhi – 110 017, India
Penguin Group (NZ)
67 Apollo Drive, Mairangi Bay, Auckland 1310, New Zealand
(a division of Pearson New Zealand Ltd)
Penguin Books (South Africa) (Pty) Ltd
24 Sturdee Avenue, Rosebank, Johannesburg 2196, South Africa

Penguin Books Ltd, Registered Offices:
80 Strand, London, WC2R 0RL, England

First published by Penguin Group (Australia), 2007

10 9 8 7 6 5 4 3 2 1

Cover and text design by Adam Laszczuk © Penguin Group (Australia)
Original concept by Jo Hunt © Penguin Group (Australia)
Cover Floral Mural in background and endpapers artwork copyright © Ebony Bizys
Cover photograph by Gary Heery
Author photograph of Saskia Havekes by Gary Heery and photograph of Gary Heery
by Jordana Maisie-Goot
All photography by Gary Heery, except image of lily pads and pink blossoms
on pages 136–137 © Australian Picture Library/Corbis

Typeset in Mrs Eaves and Frutiger by Adam Laszczuk and
Post Pre-Press Group, Brisbane, Queensland
Printed and bound in Singapore by Imago Productions
Colour reproduction by Splitting Image, Clayton, Victoria

National Library of Australia
Cataloguing-in-Publication data:

Havekes, Saskia.
    Grandiflora arrangements.

    Includes index.
    ISBN – 13: 978 192098 926 2
    ISBN – 10: 1 920989 26 9

    1. Grandiflora (Firm). 2. Flower arrangement.
    3. Flower arrangement - Pictorial works.
    I. Heery, Gary, 1949– . II. Title.

745.92

www.penguin.com.au

Stockists and Locations:

Akira Design Studio, (02) 9212 1670; www.akira.com

Anibou, (02) 9319 0655; www.anibou.com.au

Arida, (02) 9357 4788; www.arida.com.au

Billy Kwong Restaurant, (02) 9332 3300

Blinds by Bayliss, (02) 9360 7244; www.bayliss.com.au

Brunschwig & Fils, (02) 9363 4757;
www.brunschwig.com

Cavit & Co. Pty Ltd, (02) 9326 9161; www.cavitco.com

Collette Dinnigan, www.collettedinnigan.com.au

davidmetnicole, (02) 9698 7416;
www.davidmetnicole.com

Dinosaur Designs, www.dinosaurdesigns.com.au

Elizabeth Bay House, (02) 9356 3022

Establishment, (02) 9240 3000;
www.merivale.com/establishment/hotel

Howell and Howell, (02) 9328 1212

Icebergs Dining Room & Bar, (02) 9365 9000;
www.idrb.com

Ilias Design Group, (02) 9554 4188

Longrain Restaurant & Bar, (02) 9280 2888;
www.longrain.com

Lotus, (02) 9326 9000; www.merivale.com/lotus

Lynette Cunnington Chinese Art & Furniture,
(02) 9326 2227; www.chineseart.com.au

Macleay on Manning, (02) 9331 4100

Mcleod's Antiques, (02) 9361 0602

Mark Conway, (02) 9360 7806

Martyn Cook Antiques, (02) 9328 1801;
www.martyncookantiques.com

Medusa Hotel, (02) 9331 1000; www.medusa.com.au

Object: Australian Centre for Craft and Design,
(02) 9361 4555; www.object.com.au

Orientalia, (02) 9566 4461; www.orientalia.com.au

Pigott's Store, (02) 9362 8119; www.pigotts.com.au

Rose Seidler House, (02) 9989 8020

Signature Prints, (02) 8338 8400;
www.signatureprints.com.au

Tetsuya's Restaurant, (02) 9267 2900;
www.tetsuyas.com

The Country Trader, (02) 9698 4661;
www.thecountrytrader.com.au